The In-Between of Writing

The In-Between of Writing

Experience and Experiment in Drabble, Duras, and Arendt

Eleanor Honig Skoller

Ann Arbor

THE UNIVERSITY OF MICHIGAN PRESS

Copyright © by the University of Michigan Press 1993
All rights reserved
Published in the United States of America by
The University of Michigan Press
Manufactured in the United States of America

1996 1995 1994 1993   4 3 2 1

A CIP catalogue record for this book is available from the British Library.

Library of Congress Cataloging-in-Publication Data

Skoller, Eleanor Honig.
    The in-between of writing : experience and experiment in Drabble,
Duras, and Arendt / Eleanor Honig Skoller.
        p.   cm.
    Parts of chapters 2 and 3 are reprinted in rev. form from Critical
essays on Margaret Drabble (c1985) and Remains to be seen (1988).
    Includes bibliographical references and index.
    ISBN 0-472-10260-5
    1. Literature, Modern—Women authors—History and criticism.
    2. Literature, Modern—20th century—History and criticism.
    3. Women and literature. 4. Feminism and literature.
    5. Postmodernism (Literature) 6. Drabble, Margaret, 1939- —
Criticism and interpretation. 7. Duras, Marguerite—Criticism and
interpretation. 8. Arendt, Hannah. I. Title. II. Title:
Inbetween of writing.
PN471.S55 1993
809'.89287—dc20   93-27252
                                                CIP

To the memory of my mother and father

When asked, "Why don't you write the way you talk?"
Gertrude Stein replied, "Why don't you read the way I write?"

Acknowledgments

Although it is always difficult to enumerate precisely what goes into the writing of a book, some people and places have been invaluable to the development and completion of this work. The opportunity I had to participate fully in The Center for Twentieth-Century Studies during the years I spent at the University of Wisconsin–Milwaukee has had an incalculable effect on me and the kind of book that I have written.

I take great pleasure in thanking Herbert Blau for his unfailing support, from the beginning, of my desire to write in the field of ideas and of my work in this book and for the many kindnesses he has shown me over the years. I wish to thank Mary Lydon for the countless conversations we had in the early moments of the writing that helped shape the course of my thinking and for her help with some of my translations from the French; Elaine Marks for her friendship, her enthusiasm for my work, and her reading of the manuscript; Kathleen Woodward for an early reading of the manuscript and for her sustaining remarks in a close re-reading of the first chapter; Tobin Siebers for reading the manuscript and for his generous and cogent response to it; and Jeffrey Skoller, whose insights, in the final moments of the writing, helped me keep my eye on my own vision.

I thank my editor at the University of Michigan Press, LeAnn Fields, for her warm enthusiasm for the book and her thoughtful patience with me whenever I needed it.

I am very lucky to have a special group of friends who have been with me and for me throughout the writing of this text, and for that I thank them most deeply. My thanks go also to Donald S. Skoller, who has provided me with all manner of support.

I am joyfully indebted to my sons, Jeffrey, Larry, and Matthew, who have given me so many years of love and laughter—this book is my gift to them.

Parts of chapter 2 are reprinted with perimission of G. K. Hall & Co., an imprint of Macmillan Publishing Company, from *Critical Essays on Margaret Drabble,* edited by Ellen Cronan Rose. Copyright © 1985 by Ellen Cronan Rose. Part of chapter 3 appeared in *Remains to be Seen: Essays on Marguerite Duras,* edited by Sanford S. Ames (New York: Peter Lang, 1988). I am grateful to both publishing companies for permission to reprint them here in revised form.

Contents

Abbreviations

Arendt:
HC	*The Human Condition*
RV	*Rahel Varnhagen: The Life of a Jewish Woman*
MDT	*Men in Dark Times*
BPF	*Between Past and Future*
"OHA"	"On Hannah Arendt"
OR	*On Revolution*
"JP"	"The Jew as Pariah: A Hidden Tradition"
OT	*Origins of Totalitarianism*
EJ	*Eichmann in Jerusalem*

Drabble:
NE	*The Needle's Eye*
MG	*The Middle Ground*
IA	*The Ice Age*
RG	*The Realms of Gold*
W	*The Waterfall*

Duras:
RLVS	*Le ravissement de Lol V. Stein*
LP	*Les parleuses*
WW	*Woman to Woman*
L'A	*L'amant*
L	*The Lover*
DM	*Marguerite Duras à Montréal*
Hma	*Hiroshima mon amour* (French version)
HMA	*Hiroshima Mon Amour* (English translation)
YV	*Les yeux verts*
"AS"	"Aurélia Steiner"

VC	*Le vice-consul*
E	Ellenbogen's trans., *The Vice-Consul*
O	*Outside*
LD	*La douleur*

Chapter 1

But to Begin at Any Beginning at Least as a Beginning Is

In Virginia Woolf's *The Waves,* Bernard exclaims, "I need a little language such as lovers use, words of one syllable . . . . I need a howl; a cry" (295). Woolf's howl may be the undulating wail of a siren (avatar of woman/trouble) that marks the discovery of a prison break, warning that someone is loose, on the loose—free of constraints. In *Between the Acts,* she depicts the end of those whalebone bindings that encased the woman's body, when she has Mrs. Manresa say: "'And what do I do? Can I say it aloud? . . . I take off my stays . . . and roll in the grass.' She laughed wholeheartedly. She had given up dealing with her figure and thus gained freedom" (42).

Just as Woolf celebrated the demise of the corset, letting the body go, so she attempted to dissolve the mimetic stays holding language fast to the "real" world. She had already written in her diary during the composition of *The Waves,* "there must be a great freedom from 'reality'" (*A Writer's Diary* 141). As Circe warned Odysseus, the siren's sound is resisted only by restraints that are not easily overcome. Since *Between the Acts,* Woolf's last novel, written at the start of World War II, women may have gotten rid of the corset, but they have not really let themselves go—have not raised the curtain on the next act—on another scene of writing.

The feminist literary enterprise has been to write women into literary history, to make a place from which women can write, to find a voice and even a language. To reveal the misrepresentation of women in literature and the occultation of women writers by men, feminists are assiduously researching and testing the truth-value of literature against an

overwhelmingly experiential reality. In this kind of reading, it is important not only how true to life a writer's words are but how faithful (or
not) the elements of her work (plot, character, description) are to those
in her real life. Another facet of this reading strategy is the insistence of
many feminist critics on evaluating themes and portrayal according to
their usefulness (or lack of it) to the ideology of feminism, which is the
struggle for liberation (on all fronts) from patriarchal oppression and for
self-realization and self-possession (in several senses).

The struggle is necessary and has been effective, but in spite of its
liberating aims, it has caused a narrowing of the feminist purview, a kind
of monism that consists in a devotion to the authority of experience in
literary works. As Elaine Marks puts it: "Experience has become the
Divine Providence of a secular religion, the sole guarantee of authenticity
in writing and speech" ("Feminisms Wake" 102). The phrase "authority
of experience" is the name of a collection of feminist criticism edited by
Arlyn Diamond and Lee R. Edwards and is prompted by one of the
book's epigraphs: "experience, though noone auctoritee / Were in this
world, is right ynough for me / To speke." Of telling interest here is
that the mandate given for the authority of experience comes from the
Wife of Bath, who is not a real person but a character in Chaucer's *The
Canterbury Tales*—a strong filter of raw experience, indeed. This instance
reveals a paradox that feminists cannot escape: no experience can be told
without some form of mediation that renders it changed, to say nothing
of the notion that perception is always already a mediation; the truth of
communicated experience is always attenuated, undermined.

In what is now being called a "third generation" or "third moment"
in the women's movement (Kristeva, "Women's Time" 33–35; Culler,
On Deconstruction 61–64), the insistence that women's experience in the
world be written and read must now be superseded by considerations
of how that experience is being translated into innovative and critical
works, or as I would rather put it, how that experience is being translated into critically innovative and innovatively critical works—adverbial
modifications that efface the polarity but keep the conjunction between
invention and criticism. The modification makes a difference. It bespeaks
a breaking up of boundary lines, a lifting of constraints—an uncorset-
ing—that allows what is essential in any liberation effort: a freedom of
movement away from the closure of representation of "real" experience
toward the open-mindedness of experiment, or more accurately yet,
toward experimentation with open-endedness.

Commenting on Susan Sontag's "prophetic" statement in 1975, "Like all moral truths, feminism is a bit simple-minded. That is its power and . . . that is its limitation," Marks, though not necessarily agreeing that "feminism is a bit simple-minded," is convinced that feminism "must establish and maintain connections between itself and other contemporary modes of inquiry" ("Feminisms Wake" 106) to survive. Similarly, feminism and contemporary writing, by virtue of their alterity in relation to the dominant conventions, should have intersected, formed a nexus, but they have missed making that connection; at their most parochial, they have fallen far afield from one another.

Experimental prose fiction since World War II has come to be called postmodern (writing). It is among other things highly self-reflexive and frequently marked by attempts to break the old forms, blur the genres, make indistinct the line between fiction and non-fiction (criticism, history, and philosophy), and release the tension between the warring opposites characteristic of Western thought, such as inside/outside, presence/absence, truth/lie, fiction/reality, and even masculine/feminine. It is at once fluid and discursive. It would seem that such a writing would be eminently suitable to a feminist practice—inviting even. It could be that place where women would be able to articulate new visions, envision new articulations—a horizon that sparkles with possibilities. Yet there are hardly any women writers among the postmoderns, except perhaps in France, where there has been some experimentation.

It may be that postmodern writing is tainted for women writers by its discursivity, its self-reflection—distanced and distancing—because according to feminist literary theory, discursive writing is phallocentric, that is, of a masculine order. The postmodern appears to be masculine not only theoretically but empirically, as confirmed in such critical works as Ihab Hassan's *Dismemberment of Orpheus,* Annie Dillard's *Living by Fiction,* and Andreas Huyssen's *After the Great Divide,* in whose compendia of postmodern writers (or contemporary modernists, as Dillard calls them) female names are rarely seen. These lists contain the (mostly male) names of contemporary writers whose works have become part of the canon and are currently being discussed in intellectual journals, book reviews, and university classrooms throughout much of the Western world.

It is paradoxical that such a purportedly masculine endeavor dominates at the time of the cultural and political emergence of women, a time of increased visibility of women's writing—of the possibility of a women's writing. At this most propitious moment, the question "Why are there hardly any exponents of postmodernism among English-speaking women writers?" seems unavoidable. It should be noted that there are a few women whose fiction may be called postmodern. Among the better known are Renata Adler (*Speedboat, Pitchdark*), Joan Didion (*Play It as It Lays, Democracy*), and especially Kathy Acker (*Great Expectations, Blood and Guts in High School, Don Quixote, Empire of the Senseless*). The first two are primarily known as critics, essayists—commentators; the last, emerging as *the* postmodern woman writer, is also involved in the postmodern art world. Despite her desire not to be categorized, I would include Christine Brooke-Rose (*Amalgamemnon, Zorandor*), who, in addition to writing experimental novels, is a professor and literary theorist. Reaction to their fiction has been mixed and generally guarded, and rarely is any of it found on the reading lists of courses in the contemporary or postmodern novel. An exception is Ursula LeGuin, whose science fiction is appreciated and taught. In addition to these women are Mimi Albert, Marianne Hauser, Fanny Howe, Elaine Kraf, and Carole Sturm Smith, who are part of the Fiction Collective, a publishing company (whose distributor is George Braziller) made up of experimental writers among whom the most well known are Ronald Sukenick, Raymond Federman, Thomas Glynn, and Jonathan Baumbach.

That there is this scarcity of women experimenters in prose fiction—most of the experimentation by women is taking place in poetry, film, art, and performance art[1]—is actually surprising, because in the past a number of women (largely English-speaking) have written experimental prose works, most notably Virginia Woolf and Gertrude Stein, but also Dorothy Richardson, Djuna Barnes, Zora Neale Hurston, and arguably, Jean Rhys, all of whom did their major work before World War II (except for Rhys, who wrote her last novel, the acclaimed *Wide Sargasso Sea,* in 1966). They are, however, generally called modernists. Although those writers we call modernists were overwhelmingly male (the women who were experimenting at the time were not nearly as visible or as highly regarded as the men until, through the efforts of women literary critics, they were rediscovered),[2] there were some women experimenting. Among the postmodernists, we find even fewer women writers, especially in the United States and England.

In France the reverse has prevailed. There is hardly any mention of experimental women writers in the prewar period, but after the war, Marguerite Duras and Nathalie Sarraute came to be associated with the experimental writing of the fifties and sixties known as *le nouveau roman.*

In the late sixties and seventies, a group of somewhat younger writers, at first closely associated with the Paris quarterly *Tel quel,* studied and built on the *nouveau roman,* or *les recherches,* as the enterprise was called by Alain Robbe-Grillet. They, too, experimented with the practice of writing (*l'écriture*). The French press dubbed them the school of *le nouveau nouveau roman.* Associated with the *Tel quel* group was Julia Kristeva, an émigré from Bulgaria, whose work in literary criticism (focusing on such modern experimentalists as Artaud, Joyce, and Céline) was like the others at *Tel quel,* heavily informed by the new ideas, under the rubric *les sciences humaines,* that were proliferating in the French intellectual world at the time: structural linguistics and anthropology, semiology (Ferdinand de Saussure, Claude Lévi-Strauss, Roland Barthes); philosophy and history (Jacques Derrida, Michel Foucault, Gilles Deleuze); and psychoanalysis (Jacques Lacan, Serge Leclaire, Jean-François Lyotard). My approach in the readings that form the body of this book is eclectic, drawing on linguistics, semiotics (semiology), psychoanalysis, and deconstruction.

Kristeva, who has been characterized by Marks as "a loner, charting her own domain" ("Women and Literature in France" 837), has held a singular and often embattled position in the French feminist movement. Though she supports the liberation of women, her credentials as a literary feminist—devotion to sexual difference in writing—remain weak. In a 1977 interview with *Le nouvel observateur,* she declares:

> I am quite dedicated to the feminist movement but I think feminism, or any other movement, need not expect unconditional backing on the part of an intellectual woman. I think the time has come to emerge out of the "for-women-only" practice, out of a kind of mythicising of femininity. (*Desire in Language* 10)

In "Women's Time," an essay published in the United States in 1981, she writes:

> In this third attitude of women [of a third generation of concerned, active (writing) women], which I strongly advocate—which I imagine?—the very dichotomy man/woman as an opposition between two rival entities may be understood as belonging to *metaphysics.* What can "identity," even "sexual identity," mean in a new theoretical and scientific space where the very notion of identity is challenged? (33–34)

These provocative remarks notwithstanding, Kristeva has long been concerned with repression of the body of the mother (*la mère qui jouit*) in Western society, the relation of women to language, the acquisition of language by the developing infant as it differentiates itself from the mother, and the reappearance of the infant's earliest echolalia and rhythmic babble in avant-garde works, as their feminine aspect or register.

The writings of several other intellectual women became known during this time—a time that included the historic May 1968 mass demonstrations of French workers and students that helped pave the way for the MLF (*Mouvement de Libération des Femmes*). Among them are Hélène Cixous, Luce Irigaray, Michèle Montrelay, Catherine Clément, and Monique Wittig. Of these, Wittig is known primarily as a novelist, Cixous has come to be known as a dramatist and also writes novels, and Kristeva has recently written a long novel. All are professors, psychoanalysts, journalists, and critics, and all are writers. Their common concerns are language and a writing, *l'écriture féminine,* succinctly defined by Marks as "the inscription—both the markings and the traces—of women's difference in language" ("Women and Literature in France" 836). Like Kristeva, Cixous and Irigaray are influenced by the new work in *les sciences humaines*—both by Derrida, Irigaray by Lacan especially, being herself a dissident Lacanian psychoanalyst. Cixous, a literary critic and theorist, works, like Kristeva, on male experimental modernists, such as Joyce, Kafka, and Genet, and also on some poets: Shakespeare, Holderlin, Rilke, and Kleist. The one female exception to this list is her work on Clarice Lispector, a Brazilian writer. Unlike Kristeva, however, Cixous and Irigaray are both devoted to *l'écriture féminine,* to a writing that proceeds from the body, a feminine body whose libidinal economy is evident. It is a writing that purports to be close to the unconscious, that allows the unconscious to speak, a writing that designates, de-signs, designs woman. For Cixous, although her work is informed by a certain essentialism—her claim is that women do have privileged access to it— *l'écriture féminine* is not the preserve of women writers only.

Irigaray does hold to the possibility of a woman's language, certainly a woman's discourse. Her writing is even closer to the body than Cixous's (if such proximities are measurable). It speaks of body fluids, of body parts, of the plurality that is *This Sex Which is Not One* (*Ce sexe qui n'en est pas un,* the title of one of her key texts) in contradistinction to the unicity (and aridity) of the male erection: theories and phallocracies. Her interlocutors, too, are men: Lacan always, although she may not mention his name, and working backward from Freud to Plato. Irigaray and Cixous have attempted to demonstrate and argue the repression of women by a writing that is different, that bespeaks difference, that is analytical *and* poetic, personal *and* abstract, and that exudes a strong sense of spontaneity. It is a writing that tries to de-theorize (male) theoretical positions by exploding them with a torrent of language that is rarely found in theoretical/philosophical disquisitions.

Although Cixous has written short stories, novels, and plays, she is still chiefly known as a professor and literary theorist. The landmark works of Cixous and Irigaray—manifestos really—"Le rire de la méduse" and *Ce sexe . . .* , are departures from the usual "objective" or "neutral" (read phallocentric) diction and tone common to exposition. Their foray might be into a new hybrid genre of essay writing that is neither pure essay nor fiction, that may be autobiographical without being confessional—a new border that could be marked feminine. "For Cixous," writes Alice Jardine, "women would in fact seem to be, almost intrinsically, protopostmodernists" (*Gynesis* 262). Yet a certain abdication of the letter (law, philosophy, history, theology, morality, ethics) has hardened into what appears to be an eschewal of this register for women, by women, who are dedicated to the notion of sexual difference in writing especially, on the grounds that embracing it is aiding and abetting, worse, internalizing, their own oppression. Hence the neofemininity (the apotheosis of some innate essence that is woman) of *l'écriture féminine,* which tries to write itself into the *symbolic order* (a term coined by Lacan to indicate the register of language), but differently.

Monique Wittig is not partisan to the essentialism of *l'écriture féminine.* But each of her works, *L'opoponax, Les guerillères, Le corps lesbien,* and *Brouillon pour un dictionnaire des amantes* (known in the United States as *Lesbian People's Material for a Dictionary*), rewrites a major genre, redefines it, and reinvents it for women. She does so with the female bildungsroman that shows the transcendence of feminine socialization; the epic poem that sings of the military defeat of the patriarchal order by women; the myths and legends, including the Song of Songs, that are reclaimed by the lesbian lovers; and a tentative lexicon that "redefines, but does not confine words and women to narrow meanings" (Wenzel 285).

Wittig attempts to create a symbolic order that is not based on an obligatory heterosexual model, but one that refuses the notion of woman as it is understood today. The success of this enterprise is at best questionable even on feminist grounds, because if the symbolic order is coded male, to make it female, however unrestrictive, replaces one homosexuality with another. But it is a "journey through language" (Wenzel 284) and has all the earmarks of an elaborate experiment in cultural revision. It is a modernist experiment whose utopian goal is to recreate in language a new and whole woman, body and mind, (the words *utopian* and *whole* signal, respectively, transcendence and closure—however fragmented it may appear to be on the page—both tenets of literary high modernism), who lives in a society from which she is not alienated, a new order in which patriarchy has been defeated by women writers/ warriors (here women are the namers), and in which women can live together—with men if they choose—in a world from which violence has disappeared. *Les guerillères, The Lesbian Body,* and the *Dictionary* are altogether a courageous, but risky, project. The power of its polemics produces an aesthetic naïveté that is absent from her prizewinning first novel, *L'opoponax.* Her books now seem to be more controversial in feminist circles than outside them, where they are discussed only every now and then.

I am not attempting to polarize modernism and postmodernism. I do not believe that a strict opposition between the two exists. Such oppositions lead to the oversimplification and reduction of analyses. It is the relation between modernism and postmodernism that is illuminating—an idea that Huyssen demonstrates in *After the Great Divide,* his cogent study of modernism and postmodernism. Neither am I attempting, moreover, to explain modernism in any detailed or definitive way. One of my concerns here is to show that some of the well-known concepts of literary high modernism (embedded in those works that have been prized and authorized as serious literature—art) are undergoing a critique in ideas and works that can be called postmodern, and to show some aspects of the relation of women writers to both.

A final example of an apparent eschewal of the letter by women is the proliferation of confessional novels—representations of the authors' experiences written in transparent language, thinly disguised autobiographies whose best known exemplars in this country are Marilyn French's *The Women's Room* and Erica Jong's *Fear of Flying.* Concomitant with the novel of experience is the development of a *gynocritics,* "criticism concerned with *woman as writer*" (Showalter, "Towards a Feminist Poetics" 25), whose aim is to develop a criticism (on all levels) for and by women. In the foregoing examples of women who decry the letter (but want to be heard) is a discernible retreat from the world as it is—despite its emphasis on experience—to a definite policy of separatism. Not to assume the letter, not to enjoy it as a birthright as a human being among human beings, is to remain in exile, poised at the threshold, so to speak.

As far back as 1976, it seemed to Kristeva that women often stay out of the way of the new and unusual advances of our culture. She accuses women of demonstrating sentimentalism and romanticism and believes that women must be helped to understand that "new forms of discourse are harmonious with the women's cause" ("China, Women, and the Symbolic" 17). Not much had changed by 1982, when she wrote in "Women's Time" that women are still writing the same "naive whining of market place romanticism," that were it not for the feminist label, a good deal of work would have been rejected as anachronistic. She complains that too many women artists are attacking "Language and Sign as the ultimate supports of phallocratic power." Such harsh criticism notwithstanding, she is waiting for something to happen: "And yet, no matter how dubious the results of these recent productions by women, the symptom is there—women are writing, and the air is heavy with expectation: What will they write that is new?" (32).

New is the issue. Feminism feels new and has brought changes and a new awareness, but it is also a reassertion of identity (self), representation, and (transcendent) truth—another face of humanism, a bedrock of literary high modernism. It is iconoclastic, rather than radical; it seeks not to sweep these tenets away, but to sweep them out, clean them up, as it were. So, oddly, it is ultimately a conservatism. Feminism in the United States has been an effective and widespread social critique, and feminist literary studies (through which much European philosophy and theory is received) have been crucial. The effort, however, to equalize, to liberate, brings with it a touch of tyranny—to institutionalize, codify, count up, recount, essentialize, represent women's experience, and to produce a "new social subject, women" (DeLauretis, *Alice Doesn't* 186). It brings tyranny because the effort subjects and subjugates. Socially and politically, the tyrannical edge may go unnoticed in the effort, in the struggle itself (and may be necessary to the accomplishment of its objectives), but in the university and the arts—literature in particular—it hypostatizes. It inhibits a certain freedom, prevents certain liberties from being taken (or held) that could result in, at least influence, new work.

The explosion of language, its plurality, its polysemy, and its play (in its senses other than and including games) in such practioners as

Cixous and Irigaray, though it is new and exciting, is eventually tamped down by their ultimate objective: to write the body, to pulverize the woman's body and pour it onto the page. It becomes just one more representation (however new and different it may appear on the page) of that so often represented body, and for yet another reason (albeit a noble one). The (re)inscription of women in literature and history becomes a (re)inscription in the dialectics of representation—more of the same. What is newest from women writers does not quite carry them over the threshold, hence that failed connection between feminism, by any name, and postmodernism. Are feminism and postmodernism oxymoronic? Is it impossible, by definition, for them to intersect?

On both sides of the Atlantic, the question prevails: "Why are so few women writing in the postmodern vein?" To attempt an answer to this complex and gritty question, I take my cue from Hannah Arendt, who, in her treatise on thinking, emulated the strategy Wittgenstein used in his *Philosophical Investigations*. "It often happens," Wittgenstein reasons, "that we only become aware of important *facts,* if we suppress the question 'why?'; and in the course of our investigations these facts lead us to an answer" (Arendt, *The Life of the Mind* 125). Adopting this strategy, I will suppress, or defer, the question I have raised, and in an effort to probe the failure of a nexus between feminism and postmodernism, I ask instead, "What is the relation of women's experience and literary experiment?"

To explore this relation, I have selected for analysis a number of works written by three women writers: Hannah Arendt, Margaret Drabble, and Marguerite Duras. I have chosen these particular writers as much for their differences from each other as for their exemplary possibilities vis-à-vis the issues at hand. What ties them together for me is that each has a distinct relation to language and a close tie to world history that remains largely untreated in literary studies. In my view, literary feminists have virtually left Arendt unread, have misread Drabble, and have only partially read (reduced) Duras. This series of lapses is not, as I see it, the sort of creative misprision that readings have come to claim for themselves in our time—none more forcefully than feminist readings.

Because Hannah Arendt was a leading philosopher and political theorist—one of the few (until recently) major women philosophers and theorists of the twentieth century—she is a highly visible exception to the notion that women are not readily discursive or polemical in their writing without becoming men—that is, without imitating masculine forms. She was, to use her phrase, *feminini generis*. Yet she spent her life writing and thinking—indeed, she wrote a great deal about thinking, which she saw as having been abandoned in today's world in favor of action. She was deeply intellectual in her orientation to the world (although she was strongly committed to political action): "If I can be said to 'have come from anywhere,' it is from the tradition of German philosophy" (Letter to Gershom Scholem, in Feldman 246). German philosophy, a bastion of phallocratic endeavor, can hardly be considered a fit place for a woman. But Arendt claimed German philosophy as her basic formation, and an exile nonpareil—as a Jew she had to flee Germany, her homeland, to survive—she came to call the German language *der heimat* (home). To her, German was her childhood and youth, her memories: "*Muttersprache*, 'mother tongue'—[l]anguage was continuity" (Young-Bruehl 3).

Arendt loved philosophy and had a passion for abstract language. She made them the means by which she learned to understand and respond to the world. Her encounter with the world unfolded itself in a relation to language in which telling the truth was a matter of being able to generalize without falsifying (Young-Bruehl 58–59). But if abstract language is male, as some feminist theory has it, how was Arendt able to transmute her experience in the world into her writing, into that kind of language with which she had such an affinity? This sort of question is pivotal in any consideration of the relation of women's experience to their writing. Rather than think of Arendt as the exception (a condition she detested) that may prove the rule, I have chosen to use Arendt and her work as paradigmatic of the failure of current theoreticians to account for (or take into consideration) the desire of women for the symbolic order.

There has been a rather consistent effort by women to abdicate the register of the letter, by which the psyche and the culture are constituted, to men who over the centuries have claimed it as their right. The letter is the province of men, and women stand at its gates, perpetual exiles, except for an occasional interloper who may get through only to be recognized as being like a man. As Catherine Clément puts it: "Even if somewhere it is true that rhetoric and vocabulary are formed by centuries of male cultural domination, to renounce the exercise of thought, to give it to them, is to *perpetuate*, as always when it is a matter of 'not being part of the system'" (Marks and Courtivron 135). Separatism does not give rise to equality. It is generally reductive and produces barbarism. For Hannah Arendt, the letter, constitutive of her subjecthood (in all resonances of the word), was her way of being free in the world, without dispensation—of being inalienably, a woman, a Jew, a human being.

The connections between Hannah Arendt and the women's movement are not intimate. She would not engage the woman's question from as early on as the thirties, because she would not entertain the separation of women's issues from the larger range of political concerns, just as she was against the divorce of Jewish issues from national and international ones (Young-Bruehl 97). As a singular and controversial female figure in philosophy and political theory, she could have been useful to the movement. But she was unreceptive to the publicity that goes along with paving the way for others, not only because it put her in the limelight, but because of her distaste for exceptionism—whether of women, Jews, or blacks. She insisted that the exceptions of a group eventually cut themselves off from the rest, usually the poorer, less advantaged ones, and erroneously come to feel themselves exempt from the common destiny of that group (Arendt, *Rahel Varnhagen* [1959] 217).

Arendt was the first woman invited to give the Christian Gauss seminars at Princeton University, in the fall of 1953, and she was "annoyed at being cast in the role of 'token woman'" (Young-Bruehl 272). In 1959, when she was invited to join the Princeton faculty as a full professor, making her the first woman to achieve that rank there, she nearly refused the appointment because the university stressed the "first woman" aspect in their reports to the press. She did not want to be distinguished from other women because of her education, her personality, or any other virtue. She wanted women to relate the legal and political discrimination they endured to that of all groups denied equality. Her reaction to the Princeton appointment led Arendt to tell an interviewer, "I am not disturbed at all about being a woman professor because I am quite used to being a woman" (Young-Bruehl 273).

What has probably furthered Arendt's distance from the women's movement is her insistence on her unusual, puristic distinction between the social and the political. Briefly, they correspond respectively to the private and public realms, the former that of necessity, the latter that of freedom (Arendt, *The Human Condition* 30). The feminist notion that "the personal is political," current some years ago, probably would have made her quite uncomfortable. For her, only the nonpersonal (comprising that knowledge and action that everyone freely comes together to share in) is political, a notion at the bottom of which is always the Greek word *polis*—a space created for the gathering of peers. The public arena is the place where "the distance, the worldly space between men"[3] is maintained (*HC* 52). In the private realm, no such distinction exists between freely congregated people. All is based on providing and maintaining the necessities of life: food, sex, reproduction, and health. Here people strive to share the same space, to eliminate the distance between them, to create interdependence.

For Arendt, the private realm is essentially monarchical, ruled by someone who, although liberated (i.e., not forced), is not free (Arendt, *On Revolution* 30). One is free only among one's peers—in the polis. The "worldly space between men" that exists in the polis gives one a place to stand. It provides a history, a specificity, a standpoint. Only in the world do these things exist. Without that space, there is only *worldlessness* (Arendt's term), a solipsistic, inbred condition that leads nowhere, is nowhere. Although the public realm has kept women out from its inception (the domain of women has always been private), Arendt would not abandon it as the place where freedom exists. That she assumed the right of women to inhabit that space and would insist on their being legally endowed with all the rights that men have in regard to it is beyond question.

Mary O'Brien, a British feminist (one of the very few feminists to give Arendt any reading at all) would adamantly disagree with me about this. In *The Politics of Reproduction,* O'Brien reads Arendt's notion of the separation of the public and private realms through the prism of her feminist position, which considers "male philosophy an ideology of male supremacy" (5) and maintains that "political theory justifies male supremacy" (7). Her search is for a theoretical component of a feminist praxis rooted in experience located "within *the total process of human reproduction*" (8; O'Brien's emphasis). She argues that it is only with an "adequate understanding of the process of reproduction, nature's traditional and bitter trap for the suppression of women, that women can begin to understand their possibilities and their freedom" (8). Reading Arendt, clumsily in my opinion, through such a prism allows O'Brien to carelessly accuse her of "accept[ing] the normality and even the necessity of male supremacy" (100): men only "escape from the thrall of necessity" (101) and excell in the freedom of the "superior" public realm.

O'Brien is invoking a separatism based on biology that does not liberate women from being reduced to the determinism of their reproductivity.

Arendt believes that there must be two realms of existence for each human being (regardless of sex), one private, the other public, and that no one can do without both of these in order to become an individual participating in the world. The relation of both realms is seen in Arendt's remarks on love in *The Human Condition,* in which she insists that by reason of its passion, love is private, the most unworldly of states, because it destroys the space between people. Only the fruit of that love—a child—is "an in-between" that can "insert itself between the two lovers" (242). That child (male or female) is "representative of the world in that it also separates them [the lovers]; it is an indication that they will insert a new world in the existing world" (242). Arendt considers *natality* (a general condition of existence as in birth, death, natality, mortality [*HC* 8]) a cornerstone of the human condition that begins in a private realm but appears and shines forth in a public one where freedom—each birth is a new beginning—is a possibility (*HC* 7, 177). Nancy Fraser, in *Unruly Practices: Power, Discourse, and Gender in Contemporary Social Theory,* provides some important insights into the relation of the social to the public and private realms vis-à-vis gender, which I touch on in chapter 4 in some further discussion of the issues of freedom and the two realms.

The public realm, synonymous with freedom, which can be lost or forfeited, is for Arendt intimately tied up with her love of the world. Her congress with the public realm takes place in language, in writing. Though her love of the world is constituted in a language that is not lyrical or dramatic but discursive and abstract, it is inseparable from her experience in the world. Although distanced and distilled, Arendt writes herself, her autobiography, into her corpus, her theoretical work—nowhere more clearly than in *Rahel Varnhagen: The Life of a Jewish Woman.* The form that her work takes is a storytelling, as she calls it, that discloses meaning. It is a way of making sense, a thinking through, of experience: "The story reveals the meaning of what otherwise would remain an unbearable sequence of sheer happenings" (*Men in Dark Times* 104). Storytelling is for Arendt the link between thinking (*la vita contemplativa*) and action (*la vita activa*). It is "the point of departure for her concept of political thinking precisely because it respects the condition of action and does not presume to supersede it" (Hill 287). Concepts that are not rooted in experience—in the specificity of one's own natality, or to use Lacan's language, in the full acceptance of the *nom du père,* the name and the no of the father with all its interdictions and enfranchisements—lead to a highly articulated, "more or less well-equipped cloud-cuckoo land" (*MDT* 18).

Although Arendt writes her relation to the world without making up plots and characters, she does tell stories, many of which are elicited by the definitions and the etymologies of the words she uses to develop her concepts. As Mary McCarthy describes it:

> [Very] close to the roots of Hannah Arendt's thinking is the *distin-guo:* "I distinguish this from that. . . . " Each of her works is an unfolding of definitions, which of course touch on the subject, and more and more enlighten it as one distinction unfolds (after another). ("On Hannah Arendt" 337, 338)

Arendt was often criticized by her colleagues for her method of distinguishing, for her use of definitions. She was accused of giving "aesthetic pleasure" and of a "certain lack of seriousness about modern problems in much of her work" ("OHA" 307). Arendt responded to these reproofs by explaining to C. B. McPherson, a political economist who was questioning her:

> We all grow up and inherit a certain vocabulary. We then have got to examine this vocabulary. And this is not just by finding out how this word is usually used, which then gives as a result a certain number of uses. These uses are then legitimate. In my opinion a word has a much stronger relation to what it denotes or what it is, than just the way it is being used between you and me. That is, you look only to the communicative value of the word. I look to the disclosing quality. And this disclosing quality has, of course, always an historical background. ("OHA" 323)

To remember the past is to tell its story. Storytelling is a form of recollection and a way of reconciling ourselves to the past—a way of knowing who and what we are in relation to the world. Hence story and history imbricate. The world we understand is a written world—a plurality, a multiplicity of narratives. Between the particularity of one's natality and the plurality of the world lies the story: the mastering of a moment of the past, for a moment. In Lacanian language, the storyteller

becomes *le sujet supposé savoir,* the subject (who is) supposed to know—
only for the duration of the story. When the story ends, the place of
knowing is relinquished once more to the play of forces that Arendt sees
(in an interpretation of one of Kafka's aphorisms) as the fight between
past and future in which each human being carves out anew an in-
between, a gap in which to think, in which to create a present—to create
the tenses (*Between Past and Future* 11). According to Arendt:

> Mastering the past can take the form of ever-recurrent narra-
> tion. . . . The narrative has been given its place in the world, where
> it will survive us. There it can live on—one story among many.
> There is no meaning to these stories that is entirely separate from
> them. (*MDT* 21–22)

Understanding the past is no longer a matter of applying an inher-
ited set of values or ideals to a particular event and making it part of a
tradition of thought. For Arendt, no tradition can be passed on. The
wave of totalitarianism that swept over Europe with the rise of Hitler (it
had begun with the imperialism of bourgeois politics that had peaked in
the nineteenth century) and ended in the unspeakable crimes of World
War II precluded any possibility of passing down a tradition of thought
by which people could live and interpret the events of the world. "The
thread of tradition is broken," writes Arendt, "and we must discover the
past for ourselves—that is, read its authors as though nobody has ever
read them before" (*BPF* 204). Stan Spyros Draenos, writing on Arendt,
calls such reading and thinking "groundless" (209–24). There are no
eschatologies, teleologies, or transcendent truths. Arendt calls this condition "thinking without a bannister" ("OHA" 336). There is nothing
to hold on to. The great ideologies that promise, that resort to gaining
commitment from people, by whatever means it takes, have become the
fictions of humankind, of history. To paraphrase the title of an essay on
her work by Melvyn J. Hill, there are no "fictions of mankind," only
"stories of men" (275). Arendt declares that "no philosophy, no analysis,
no aphorism, be it ever so profound, can compare in intensity and rich-
ness of meaning with a properly narrated story" (*MDT* 22).

In a trenchant reading of Walter Benjamin's work in her introduction to his collection of essays called *Illuminations,* Arendt gives us much
of her understanding of experience, history, and language. The element
of experience in Arendt's story writing is essential, but that experience

is not always immediately apparent. For Arendt, experience is not so much what has happened but what it means—what can be discovered, found (out), from a narration of an event. The etymological connections between discovery, finding, and invention are luminously insistent here and reveal Arendt's affinity with the literary world and the centrality of language to her work (*MDT* 204). As Hill writes, "Stories are always inventions or, as Hannah Arendt preferred to say, discoveries" (297). We both discover and invent experience through the telling, the writing, of experience. The emphasis is on language, on writing, not as an instrumentality but as the way the world—and the subject of writing—is constituted and known. She might not have used Derridean terms, but she shared with Benjamin the belief that as we live in the world, the way we come to know that world is in a delaying, deferring process (*différance*) that is writing, that is always a scene of writing. In Derrida's words:

> the subject of writing is a system of relations between strata: of the Mystic Pad [a child's writing toy which Freud used as a model of the memory system], of the psyche, of society, of the world. . . . writing is the stage [*scène*] of history and the play of the world. ("Freud and the Scene of Writing" 113, 116)

On that stage and in that play of relations, I propose to read Hannah Arendt, Margaret Drabble, and Marguerite Duras. It is a scene in which the play of difference is grounded in memory and given in writing.

The relation of the world and psyche, of memory and writing—the present writing and the past literary tradition—is articulated in Margaret Drabble's writing style. From the north of England, she was graduated from Cambridge with a double first in English literature, with a strong interest in philosophy and metaphysics. She is now in her early fifties and has produced, among other writings, twelve novels between 1963 and 1991. She has succeeded in the difficult task of writing prose about women's experience in community with men that is readable (and misreadable) with or without access to the pervasive irony and literary parody with which her writing is laced. Hers is a double-tracked prose—an old, venerable part of the English tradition, a tradition she has fully absorbed. Yet each of her novels is so convincing as a good old-fashioned read that her critics are often apt to dismiss her as simply a "middlebrowed" (Rose, *Critical Essays* 54) chronicler of contemporary English life. Though feminist critics do not dismiss her, they take her words at face value, and many see her work as having no redeeming social value for feminism.

In my view, Drabble is a feminist in mufti, that is, one not easily recognized by current feminist checklists. She is accused, for instance, of allowing some of her heroines to be "trapped" by maternity, or even worse, to succumb to the condition of marriage, as in the case of Rose Vassiliou in *The Needle's Eye*. Rose resumes a marriage with a man who abused her and whom she does not love, for the sake of the children. Ellen Cronan Rose sees Drabble's feminism as equivocal, as either feminist or humanist, one aspect appearing, depending on which the reader reads as manifest, while the other is subliminally absorbed (*Critical Essays* 127). Cronan Rose asks for a future Drabble work that will be "an unequivocally feminist blueprint" (*Critical Essays* 129). On the contrary, I find Drabble to be pondering, meditating, questioning the old humanist values. She looks for them, would like to find them perhaps, but comes up short. At the same time, her feminism runs out of parochial steam because she sees men as no less battered by experience than women and thinks not only that women are victimized by their experience at the hands of patriarchy but that they as well as men are subject to the exigencies of world history. The festering sores on the world (and national) scenes intrude in her later novels especially: Africa, the Middle East, racism, the population explosion, poverty, crime, terrorism, and more, the gamut, to say nothing of the continual mulling over of ethical and moral precepts and behavior, and the persistent discussion of plan and accident—a virtual celebration of the letter and interrogation of the law—all of which are the concern of her women as well as her men characters. Drabble, under the guise of writing novels of interest to women, has been writing novels in which women's experience and points of view are injected into what can be called the man's world—a world that she will not relinquish to them.

This world that men and women share in her novels is no Garden of Eden or utopia. It is inevitably complicated by the difference between the sexes. As Kate Armstrong puts it in Drabble's *The Middle Ground*: "Men and women can never be close. They can hardly speak to one another in the same language. But they are compelled, forever, to try" (236). Drabble's novelistic landscape is also complicated by sex itself, a relation that is perhaps a nonrelation. It is littered with divorces and loveless marriages. They reflect a condition curiously similar to Lacan's assertion that "love rarely comes true, as each of us knows, and it only lasts for a time. For what is love other than banging one's head against a wall, since *there is no sexual relation?*" (Mitchell and Rose; my emphasis 170). Or as Lacan puts it elsewhere, "the relation between the sexes does not take place" (Mitchell and Rose 138). The key word here is *relation.* Lacan, entirely faithful to Freud, believes that sexuality is displaced from the lower parts (the genitals) and is always available (coursing) over the entire body, but that, as Clément explains it, it "does not give rise to 'intercourse' in the logical sense of the word. Nor is there exchange, [or] 'relationship'" (*Lives and Legends* 64–65). On an unconscious level, it is oneself (or that lost oneness) that one desires in the other (*Lives and Legends* 98–101). Yet for Drabble this impossible relation between men and women must continue. There must be coexistence, a standoff that allows friendship and community to flourish. A notion of Augustinian love of neighbor, and by extension, neighborhood, country, and world—not unlike that of Arendt's *amor mundi* in some respects—pervades her works.

Besides all the sex and adultery in Drabble's novels, there is also abstinence. However imminent it might appear, Rose Vassiliou and Simon Camish (*The Needle's Eye*) do not have an affair. Nor do Kate Armstrong and Hugo Mainwaring (*The Middle Ground*). There is a great deal of distance and difference between her world-sharing men and women. Alison Murray and Anthony Keating (*The Ice Age*) are in love, live together, and share responsibilities, but they do not really intersect. Rather they butt up against one another. Frances Wingate and Karel Schmidt (*The Realms of Gold*), as much as they may love each other, imagine and perceive things differently—an observation with which Drabble ends the book. Frances and Karel have just spent the evening with her cousin David Ollerenshaw: "On the way home she said to Karel, what a surprising place. But Karel didn't know what she was talking about. David's place hadn't surprised him at all" (*RG* 236). Drabble's reader gets the impression, as did Freud (in another, germane context), that men and women are a phase apart psychologically ("Femininity" 118). But they do live together, even if they can only "reach for each other in the end and fall asleep in a communion of loss," as Rose puts it in *The Needle's Eye* (112). The impossibility of complete identity with another, of total union, of sexual relation, of knowing someone else however close—parents and children, siblings, husbands and wives, lov-

ers—is a human condition—and a non-Romantic view—that Drabble
rehearses throughout her oeuvre. But friendships in her novels are vital
and long-standing. *The Radiant Way,* for example, is about three women
who met in college and have continued their friendship for some twenty-
five years, and we again follow them in *A Natural Curiosity* and *Gates of
Ivory,* the three loosely comprising a trilogy, Drabble's last three books.

No matter how many inroads women make into the male world,
how many roles they take on, their concern with the commitment to
caring, to maternity, to others in general, is evident in Drabble's novels.
She attempts to give the physiological, sociological, and psychological
details that pertain to women the same kind of matter-of-fact (neutral)
importance as those pertaining to males. The men, at the same time,
move closer to the world of women, and in some cases take on female
roles: Simon loves listening to Rose and her friend Emily Offenbach's
lengthy conversations; James Otford (*The Waterfall*) becomes Jane Gray's
nurse as she recovers from childbirth; and Anthony takes care of Alison's
severely dependent child afflicted with cerebral palsy, begins to enjoy it,
and is proud of how good he is at it. Of her several male protagonists,
Drabble writes strong portraits of their mothers (Simon's, James's, and
Hugo's), portraits that tend to even the power scales: men are as much
victims or products of their mothers as women are of the male hegemony.

No one gets off with impunity. Drabble is actually more subversive
of standard male literary practice than other writers more readily called
feminist, and she is so by more effectively moving women and the
power of their experience into the neutral (read masculine) norms of
literary description and writing in general. A menstruating woman (Alison Murray) who is in need of some protective supplies from a drugstore
she sees in the distance and is trying to get there on foot by crossing a
complex traffic circle whose lanes vehemently forbid pedestrians powerfully demonstrates the inhospitality and inhumanity of that "man-
made" construction (*IA* 172–73). This is a typical Drabble gesture (reminiscent of the Brechtian gest)—a realistic female detail coming up against
an increasingly difficult environment that she (and everyone else) has to
negotiate. Hence her choice of Yeats's moving words as epigraph to *The
Needle's Eye:* "The fascination of what's difficult / Has dried the sap out
of my veins, and rent / My heart from all its natural content."

The Drabble gests are powerful as recounted experience. Yet for
her that is the problem: how does one recount experience, give an account of it, without misrepresenting, lying? This problem is a major

theme of *The Waterfall* (and of most of her other novels as well to one degree or another). How does one get at the truth in an indeterminate world that ultimately eludes summary, that can no longer be adequately represented? In *The Middle Ground,* Kate Armstrong, a newspaper writer of feminist issues, learns as a child about telling stories by inventing a game called Confessions that made her immensely popular among the girls. She was by far the best at it, having lots of family material to go on.

> Her Mum, her Dad, Peter [her brother], Grandpa Fletcher at Abbey Wood, Arblay Street, the secrets of her body, what old Mr. Bly had tried to do to her when she went to pick up the groceries, Aunt Janey's spaniel, the sewage works [of which her father was in charge], out they all came *translated into art.* It was kind of magic, *turning shit into gold,* or so she now tells us. (23; my emphasis)

Something is always lost in translation, but something is usually gained as well. Understanding, perhaps? Insight? And what of poor truth? It fades at every grasp, yet it hovers, always waiting to be inscribed, as journalist Hugo Mainwaring (*The Middle Ground*) discovers when trying to write a novel about himself: "The more I try to tell the truth, the worse I write" (164). What is difficult is "to risk a true account," as Drabble's narrator puts it in *The Waterfall* (110), after having admitted to telling two lies about the circumstances of her estranged husband's departure. It comes down to a matter of more art: "The art of selection. The art of omission" (*MG* 183). Telling the whole story or the real story is as difficult as discerning the overall pattern that shapes the world and events. "Shapeless diversity, what was wrong with that," muses Kate to herself in *The Middle Ground* (230), which engages just that question.

The Middle Ground is far from shapeless but appears to lack form. It moves from one character's point of view to another's in a group of people connected to Kate much in the manner of Virginia Woolf's *To the Lighthouse,* except that it does not have the formal closure of Woolf's novel. Having progressed only slightly from where it began, *The Middle Ground* could just as well go on as stop. In an essay on it, Pamela S. Bromberg writes that Drabble "has foresworn the conventional well-made novel in favor of the experimental, the antinovel that punctures its own pretenses and yields no definite answers" (479).

When one reads Drabble's language carefully, allowing it to come to the foreground, to take center stage along with the events and characters, the meditation on those events and characters becomes evident as a formal device. For example, when Kate goes back to her childhood neighborhood while gathering material for a television film about women's choices in life today compared to twenty-five years ago, she begins to have some Proustian recollections about her childhood that lead her nowhere.

> The dirty, tangled roots of childhood twisted back forever and ever, beyond all knowing. Impacted, interwoven, scrubby, interlocked, fibrous, cankerous, tuberous, ancient, matted. Back in the artificial pleasure ground, the dear solitary, carefully nurtured groups of saplings stood and shivered in loneliness, straight and slim, sad and forlorn. Their roots in artificial loam, reared in artificial fibre pots, carefully separate. Tastefully arranged, fruitlessly deployed. (*MG* 132)

In the overt comparison of two kinds of roots, those of childhood and those of trees started and planted in artificial soil, is an embedded metaphor of childhood as old trees with huge root systems used in an implicit comparison between the old, ingrown, overgrown neighborhood that just grew, and the new, preplanned surfaces of a "twentieth-century paradise, pleasure gardens of concrete, lakes where land had once been, civic landscape-gardening" (*MG* 112). At the same time, Drabble is comparing life and art, describing a past that may be hidden, lost, but is not really past at all, only unreproducible and mostly incomprehensible. The words she uses in the passage have cadence, rhyme, and alliteration that produces a euphonious and visual effect that virtually illustrates the idea she is writing about. Hence not just the meditation on experience comes to the foreground but the mediation of that experience—the difference between the two words comes down to a *t,* a matter of letters. In writing, Drabble attempts to negotiate a precarious world despite its unremitting randomness.

How to negotiate such a world in writing is what Drabble writes about. Her novels, the later ones especially, are explorations of the terms of that negotiation as they play themselves out in a parody of plot and genre that is a repudiation of high modernist artists, such as Flaubert, Zola, Joyce, and Conrad—realists who, to find the truth, are determined to create an aesthetic, essential reality (more real than Real) on the page (Flaubert spent hours, days, finding *le mot juste,* and Joyce spent a day finding the right order for two sentences) and whose narratives are intended to be objective. They stand above their texts, godlike and invisible, indifferent—paring their fingernails, to invoke Joyce's famous formulation. On the contrary, what Drabble knows, what is difficult to know, or what cannot be known is out there to be grappled with by her characters, her readers, and herself, and nobody has all the right answers—or any answers.

Drabble attempts to meet the world and comprehend it by presenting her characters (mainly women in the early novels, men as well in the later ones) as caught (up) in the movement of their everyday lives, in the details of their daily concerns, in "the mysteriousness of the usual" in which they are subject to a cruel necessity.[4] She mitigates that heavy hand, however, by showing us characters grappling with their lives as if they were free to choose and do exactly as they want. In some cases, although they would not have chosen the circumstances in which they find themselves, they may decide to think of them as occurring as a result of choice rather than submit to or appear to submit to fate. Eventually we are never sure just where the *as if* is operating, and we do not get any indications or signposts from Drabble. The condition of irony prevails. She does not reveal herself, and where the reader thinks she does, he or she must be wary, for at any given moment, the author may be presenting just another point of view that should not necessarily be taken as hers.

Drabble's work contains her continual accounting of her characters' experiences in the world in tandem with her reflections on those experiences, until the opposition between choice and destiny, and that between showing—the high modernist art of literary representation—and telling—not art, but writing—are eroded, leaving a weave of language that does not represent reality but is a try at apprehending both the microcosmic and macrocosmic views of (a) life at a particular moment (also Arendt's enterprise in *Rahel Varnhagen* and Duras's in *Hiroshima mon amour,* among other texts). The result is a distancing, a surfacing of the writing. Drabble's is a heavily patterned surface, a sumptuous textile on which the play of language is there to be read or not. That play, both visible and invisible, provides not only a rich complexity of vision in her work but a comic vein that is woven into the seriousness of her subject matter. Her comedy (which I discuss more fully in chapter 2) and her

irony are often not seen or emphasized—are not usually read—in Drabble criticism, although it is with both that she stages her scene of writing,
a scene saturated with world history.

There have been too few women players in that scene, and perhaps
because of that, it has become one (in) which literary feminists have
tacitly and ironically refused to enter. It has left them, as Arendt would
say, worldless, despite all the experiences they are accumulating and
committing to paper. Attention to the scene of writing as it is disclosed
through the language—the letter—of each writer here under discussion
reveals meaning in their work that otherwise remains unread. In the
exercise of writing, we find a certain trying on or out, an essaying, of
experience—a writing practice that bespeaks experiment.[5] The rich etymological connections of these words lead to the rehearsal of their relation throughout these pages.

Marguerite Duras, in contrast with Drabble, is considered everywhere
to be an experimental writer, especially since the publication of *Le ravissement de Lol V. Stein* in 1964. Ten years later, with the publication in
France of *Les parleuses,* a series of interviews (lengthy conversations
really) with writer Xavière Gauthier that was very well received by the
French press at the time and that had a considerable impact on the MLF,
Duras became the premiere "feminist" experimental writer. She may
not have courted the label feminist, but she did not refuse it either: she
provided a positive image of/for the woman writer, and of women's use
of language (Duras and Gauthier, Jensen's trans. 191). With her remarks
in *Les parleuses* (finally translated in 1987 as *Woman to Woman*), her more
difficult works were (re)contextualized, were made more accessible,
were being read and reread through the prism of those conversations.

Being an experimental writer is difficult enough in today's world
of letters, but to be an experimental *woman* writer is to underwrite one's
own marginality, although at age seventy-eight, Duras is now among
the most celebrated writers in France. Christine Brooke-Rose, an experimental woman writer, asks for a removal of labels, especially that of
woman writer (interestingly, in French there is no feminine form for the
word *writer* [*écrivain*]): "It seems to me that the combination of woman
+ artist + experimental means so much hard work and heartbreak and
isolation that there must be little time or energy for crying out loud"
(65–66). Duras spent a lifetime writing before she was acknowledged as
a major figure. She was seventy when she won the Prix de Goncourt in

1984 for *L'amant*, another rendering of autobiographical material that had appeared in earlier texts, *Un barrage contre le Pacific* (1950) and *L'Eden Cinéma* (1977).

Duras was born Marguerite Donnadieu in 1914 in French Indochina, today called Vietnam. The daughter of colonials Henri Donnadieu, professor of mathematics, and Marie, née LeGrand, teacher, she spent all her childhood, much of it in poverty, in Indochina (with only brief visits to France) with her mother and two older brothers, her father having died when she was four. She studied at the lycée in Saigon and at eighteen moved to Paris, where she studied law and political science and received degrees in both. She eventually abandoned the name of her father and took on a place name after a village in the Lot-et-Garonne where her father had some property. She signed herself Duras—endured as Duras, *"un écrivain du désir"* (writer of desire), as she recently put it in a television interview when asked what kind of writer she was.

Desire, *the* Lacanian field, is Duras's as well, as acknowledged by Lacan, who believed, along with Freud, that the artist precedes him, paves the way for the psychoanalyst ("Hommage" 124). Duras's work is saturated with a profound sense of loss, a great lack, and is inscribed with an insistent desire for an originary plenitude, for that desperate paradise, for oneness with the mother, or to put it in strict Lacanian terms, for that lost object, *le petit objet a*. For Duras, this desire is the pain, the anguish, of writing. She writes that after many years, her mother, who at times had been quite mad, "became cursive writing" (*The Lover* 29). In the writing, through the writing, readers feel the anguish and the loss. Xavière Gauthier writes on reading Duras, "I know that when I read your books, it puts me into a state that's very . . . very strong, and that I am very uncomfortable, and that it's very hard to speak or do anything after reading them." Michel Foucault writes:

> The reading [of Duras] that I have done always makes a very strong impression on me. The presence in Marguerite Duras's work remains very intense, and yet the minute I try to talk about it, it all seems to escape me. A kind of naked force that is slippery, that one's hands cannot grasp. It's the presence of that force, that mobile and smooth force, it's that presence, vanishing at the same time, that I am prevented from talking about, and to which I am undoubtedly bound.

Hélène Cixous writes:

> I went back to all of Marguerite Duras's texts that I have read
> several times before and said to myself naively: I know them well.
> But you cannot know Marguerite Duras, you cannot grab hold of
> her. I say to myself: I've read, but it seems to me I haven't "re-
> tained." Perhaps that's it: there is a *Duras effect* and this *Duras effect*
> is something very potent that seeps out. . . . In regard to a certain
> effusion, she makes me aware of something that is almost beyond
> the text though it is *an effect of its style* [my emphasis].[6]

I have given so much testimonial here to show how pervasive the
power of Duras's work is. Each of these readers seems to be saying that
the effect of the writing, which really can only be described by an inability to describe it in any other than such vague terms as "très fort," is,
paradoxically, as elusive as it is potent, and that it is finally unnamable
except as the "Duras effect." Her writing and its effects are so singular
that it is difficult to separate them from her name. As Elizabeth Hardwick wrote of Billie Holiday, "Somehow she had retrieved from dark-
ness the miracle of pure style" (37).
   It is as if Duras were born to write, were written already before.
"L'histoire de ma vie n'existe pas," claims Duras. "Ça n'existe pas. Il n'y
a jamais de centre. Pas de chemin, pas de ligne" (*L'A* 8). (The story of
my life doesn't exist. It does not exist. There's never a center. No path,
no line.)[7] She knows "that if it's not, each time, all things confounded
into one through some inexpressible essence, then writing is nothing but
advertisement [*publicité*]" (*L* 8). That "inexpressible essence" is the desire
for the lost image that might have existed, that was omitted or forgotten,
that is not there. The strength, the *vertu* of that image, of representing
an absolute, of being the inventor of it, lies in its failure to have been
created (*L'A* 17). Duras's writing is about making barely present what
generally remains absent. "Je la laisse dans un état pantelant, la phrase"
(I leave the sentence gasping), she said once in an interview (*Marguerite
Duras à Montréal* 64).
   Duras's writing is also about its relation to her life in the world, to
her constitution as a (writing) subject—a subject that she has "fissured"
(*lezardé* [*WW* 5]). She negotiates a world full of pain and death with her
writing—her stories of forgotten love. Writing is her way of being in the
world. Rather than writing the body—an idea that Duras can no longer

stand to hear women utter (*Le Camion* 105)—she writes the boundary between the body and the world, between the inside and the outside. She says what is unsayable, writes what is unrepresentable, which is why her work is both so elusive and so strong, so resistant to categorization, the "Duras effect," indeed.

With the writing of *Le ravissement de Lol V. Stein,* Duras's work became increasingly experimental—enigmatic, perplexing, and often brief. She realized later that while writing *Le ravissement,* she had come to experience a certain fear as she wrote. She had experienced it to some degree with *Moderato Cantabile,* a novella she had written just prior to *Le ravissement.* There begins to appear some sort of omission. She has tried with considerable difficulty to explain it: "I was experimenting with this blank in the [syntactical] chain" (*WW* 4). ("J'expérimentais ce blanc dans la chaine" [*LP* 15]). She has said repeatedly that she cannot be any more explicit. Gauthier and other women have suggested that these blanks or spaces in her texts are marked as feminine, to which Duras responds variously, sometimes positively, usually indecisively with "who knows?" (*WW* 2). All she will claim is that "we could say: these books are painful to write and to read, and this pain should lead us toward a place . . . a place of experimentation" (*WW* 6), and that "basically what I do . . . what happens to me is maybe just . . . that: an experience that I let happen . . . do you think so? [She is addressing Gauthier.] Maybe it's just . . . really just . . . one [experience] that takes effect" (*WW* 7; all ellipses in this quotation are in the text except the last). Experience here is twofold: what happens to the writer both before and during the writing. Furthermore, the reader discovers, or finds, those experiences as an effect of the writing, as does the writer when she returns to her text as a reader.

For Duras, experience has never been simply "sheer occurrence." The experience is not really there for her until it goes through that transgression that she calls *un filtre,* which is the writing itself (*DM* 58). In *L'amant* she writes that her crossing of the river—literally the Mekong, figuratively both the loss of her virginity and the breaking of the racial codes when she took a Chinese lover at fifteen and a half—was "l'*experiment*" (*L'A* 16). The word is italicized, indicating that Duras has used the English word; there is no such French word. Barbara Bray, translator of *The Lover,* gives us *experience* as the equivalent. For "Tout a commencé de cette façon pour moi, par ce visage voyant, exténué, ces yeux cernés en avance sur le temps, l'*experiment*" (*L'A* 15–16), she has, "That was how everything started for me—with that flagrant, exhausted face, those rings around the eyes, in advance of time and experience" (*L* 9). I would have chosen to render it as, "It all started for me that way, the experiment, ahead of time with that flagrant, exhausted face, those rings around the eyes." With some consistency, Bray again translates that same word as a version of "experience." For "Cela, de même, je l'ai su avant l'*experiment*" (*L'A* 28), she has, "That too I knew before I experienced it" (*L* 19). My reading is, "That too I knew before the experiment." I suggest that Bray reasonably errs here in favor of some kind of a priori knowledge on the part of the girl—there is some evidence that Duras is suggesting this—and a more conventional relation between experience and experiment that is not operative for Duras, for whom experience is not simply anterior to writing.

Duras said recently that a writer writes, without necessarily writing something. In "To Write: An Intransitive Verb?" Roland Barthes suggests that writing is not simply a product of the author's but becomes "the field of the writer" in which the writer, the writing, and the field are produced at the same time (141–43). Duras's life was as much an experiment for her as the writing, and in the writing—a *field* of experimentation" ("un *champ* d'expérimentation" [*LP* 18])—the experience is found, invented. Experience, in its more ordinary guise, is forgotten, as Duras frequently reminds us, remembered in its repetition—writing is born of the forgotten. These ideas are developed in some detail in chapter 3.

Duras began making her own films around 1966, after having written several screenplays, including *Hiroshima mon amour* for Alain Resnais's film. Her films are also experimental, but for her, the privileged creative act is writing. Writing is the unknown. She never knows what the book is going to be, what she is going to write. If one does know, she insists, one does not write. When she makes a film, it is as if she sees it already done. It has already been conceptualized; she is in the position of the spectator. With writing, "Je suis donc *devant*" (I am before [it]); with a film, "Je suis *après*... " (I am after...) (*DM* 21). With a film, she finds herself in a safe, secure place that bores her. When she writes, she is "in a state of madness" (dans un état de folie [*DM* 22]). This madness is not that ascribed to women, both writers and characters, that identifies and silences them. She does not see these attributes—madness and silence—as necessarily comprising a women's literature. She has declared: "Je ne crois pas qu'il y ait une littérature de femme. Il y a des femmes"

(*DM* 51). (I don't believe that there is a woman's literature. There are only women.)

Duras does believe that women who are writers may write some things that men often do not. For instance, she has some of her characters shriek in her texts, as the vice-consul does in her novel of the same name. Of this, she says, "Je les [gens] fais crier, parce que je suis une femme, les hommes n'oseraient pas le faire. Les hommes n'auraient pas osé faire crier le vice-consul comme il crie" (*DM* 50). (I make them [people] scream because I am a woman, the men wouldn't dare to do it. Men wouldn't have dared to make the vice-consul scream as he does.) Perhaps Duras, in a different, later time and place, was able to let go of the words for a moment and find that "cry" for which Woolf's Bernard in *The Waves* so yearned. Men, she insists, would immediately speak of a sense of decency (propriety) or indecency (*décence ou indécence*) in regard to making a man shriek or scream. She gets away from this decency by writing and making her films where she is (in) the indecent: "Moi, l'indécence" (*DM* 50). She does not know if this indecency, this impropriety in which she resides when she works, is a result of being a woman artist, but she thinks that she would not do any work if she were confined to the decent, the proper. She says, "C'est le seul point féministe peut-être auquel je peux faire allusion" (*DM* 50). (It's the only feminist point, perhaps, to which I can make any allusion.)

Duras began publishing novels in 1943. Her early works have been considered to be in the "American manner" à la Hemingway (Cismaru 35), an ironic association for a writer who later became such an emblem for feminist/feminine writing. In the fifties and sixties, she was published by Editions Minuit, the house that made the *nouveau roman* famous, and she became associated with that movement. As the sixties came to a close, she was already known as an experimenter and is now spoken of in connection with Beckett (Ames, "Edging the Shadow" 17). Surprisingly, perhaps, she is not often associated with women writers, although Anne Callahan has provocatively connected her with Colette in a discussion of *La vagabonde* and *L'amant*. Calling them "pleasure's vagabonds" (202), Callahan points to the language of sensual pleasure in both these texts, a state of madness induced by the pleasure of love that recurs during the writing (202–3). According to Michèle Montrelay, feminine *jouissance* can be understood as writing (99).

Until recently, not much was known on this side of the Atlantic about Duras, although strong Anglo and American elements have always run through her work, not the least of which are the English titles—*India Song,* for example—and names of places and characters she has used. In her screenplay *Hiroshima mon amour,* she uses the name of the French city Nevers to exploit all the possibilities of that word homophonically and visually. Nevers, pronounced "Nevaire" in French, is recognizable to the ear and to the eye on the page as the English *never.* With the superimposition of the story of Nevers onto Hiroshima in the screenplay, the echo of "Never again!" silently resounds throughout the film in the repetition of the word. Attention to the words and the letters of her texts is essential to any reading of her work—her work from *La vie tranquille* (1944) to *Savannah Bay* (1983) can be read as "the progress of a letter" (Ames, "Cinderella's Slipper" 247).

Duras believes words have a far greater potency than visual images (*DM* 45). She has the ability to invest some of the words she uses with a kind of (emotional) power that makes them seem to take on a certain kind of transcendence in her work. These words in her hands become spaces that contain history, *l'histoire.* The interplay between story and history, which in French is the same word, is pivotal to my reading of Duras. In the story, the writing, she seems to translate history into emotion.

One of the most potent words in Duras's vocabulary is the word *Jew:* "Le mot juif dit en même temps la puissance de mort que l'homme peut s'octroyer et sa reconnaissance par nous" (*Les yeux verts* 86). (The word Jew stands alone in the death-dealing power that man may arrogate to himself and our recognition of that power.) In "Aurélia Steiner," as the sailor with the black hair makes love to her, Aurélia Steiner has him say over and over (without telling him what they mean) the words "Juden, Juden Aurélia, Juden Aurélia Steiner" ("AS" 164). Aurélia Steiner was born under the floorboards of a concentration camp as her mother died. Her father was hanged in that concentration camp, "dans le rectangle blanc de la cour de rassemblement" (in the white rectangle of the assembly grounds ["AS" 151]), for stealing some soup for his love, her mother, so she, their infant, would live. Because he was so thin and light, he hung there, wriggling at the end of the rope, for three days. What Aurélia Steiner has left of this *liebestod,* is the name of her dead mother, Aurélia Steiner. "La mer" is the only mother she has known: "J'écoutais les cris de la mer" ("AS" 151). "Le rectangle blanc" is a space of death and love out of which Aurélia Steiner was born. When the sailor calls her "Juden" in the heat of passion, Duras gives us another scene of *ravissement:* the body of Aurélia Steiner allows itself to be taken, carried away—ravished—by the force of the curse that holds sway over the race. When he becomes intoxicated with desire, the word displaces him and becomes a word of madness, a word that lovers cry in the madness of desire: "Aurélia Steiner coïncide avec ce mot, elle jouit avec ce mot elle rejoint complètement les amants du rectangle blanc de la mort avec ce mot" (*YV* 57). (Aurélia Steiner corresponds to this word, she comes with this word, she once again joins, completely, the lovers in the white rectangle of death with this word.)

For Duras, "le rectangle blanc" is not a universal space, but "le lieu juif" (*YV* 85). It remains a mystery to her that other people do not see it as she does. The death of a Jew at Auschwitz, for her, completely fills the history of our time (*YV* 85)—a time whose horrors she lived through: "l'histoire des Juifs, c'est mon histoire . . . [a]lors j'ai osé écrire sur les Juifs." (*DM* 73). (The history of the Jews is my history . . . so I dare to write about the Jews.) But as she points out, she does not speak about Jews; she speaks about someone who calls herself Aurélia Steiner who is Jewish. She also does not speak about Hiroshima directly in *Hiroshima mon amour;* she does so indirectly. She experiments and finds—(re)invents—in the writing the "truth" of that horrendous experience that was the war (see chapter 3 for my reading of *Hiroshima mon amour*). "Le rectangle blanc" does not stand for anything in the sense of a symbol. Rather, it becomes, in its repetition throughout the text, a hole, as Duras calls it, a space that is filled with death—murder—and love and the "Aurélia Steiner" texts.

Le rectangle blanc is also *la page blanche* on which a writer writes (*YV* 85). In the pages of Elie Wiesel's *La nuit,* an account of his experience in the camps, Duras first "saw" *le rectangle blanc,* a written space, a space of writing from which she cannot seem to escape, and which finds its way into several of her texts in different guises. On her white pages, she writes of outsiders, some women, some not, each different, other—Jews. The names hardly vary; they sound alike: Aurélia Steiner, Anne-Marie Stretter (*Le vice-consul*), Lol V. Stein (*Le ravissement*). "Oui, juive, je crois" (Yes, Jewish, I believe), Duras responded when asked (*YV* 76), although, with the exception of the "Aurélia Steiner" texts, she is careful to point out that she does not say so in the works themselves. "Le vice-consul aussi, était juif. Le vice-consul que j'ai connu, juif" (*YV* 76). (The vice-consul, too, was Jewish. The vice-consul that I knew: Jewish.)

Although she does not mention it in *Le vice-consul*, in my reading of that novel (in chapter 3) I discover it in those written spaces—those words— on *les pages blanches* of her text. Reading them, I, like the girl crossing the river, come to know it before (given) knowledge of it; I, too, experiment. Writing one's reading may verge on the experimental.

After winning the Prix de Goncourt and the Ritz Paris Hemingway Award for *L'amant*, Duras saw no reason not to publish or rerelease earlier writings, many of which she wrote for newspapers—writings of the moment, as the subtitle to her collection, *Papiers d'un jour*, indicates. She writes these writings, done between books, from what she calls the inside. Her collection, to which she gave the English title *Outside*, appeared in 1984; the English translation came out in 1986. The title is prompted by her understanding of the inside/outside relation in regard to writing: "De temps en temps j'écrivais pour le dehors, quand le dehors me submergeait, quand il y avait des choses qui me rendaient folle, outside, dans la rue—ou que je n'avais rien de mieux à faire. Ça arrivait (O 11). (From time to time I wrote for the outside world, when the outside world overwhelmed me, when things *outside*, in the street, drove me crazy—or else I had nothing better to do. Which happened. [Goldhammer's trans. ix–x].)

The second part of *Outside, La douleur*, was published in 1985. It was translated as *The War: A Memoir*. Duras has said that she found this journal in two notebooks in a blue armoire at her home in Neauphle-le-Chateau, and that she has no memory of having written it. She knows she did it, because she recognizes her handwriting and remembers the details of the events she recounts. She writes that *La douleur* is one of the most important things in her life and that "it can't really be called 'writing'" (*LD* 10). These contradictions, these matters of remembering and forgetting are indicative of her attitude toward her writing and its relation to the experiences in her life. The harrowing memoir gives us what amounts to the primal scene in relation to most of the texts she wrote afterward: *Hiroshima mon amour, Le ravissement de Lol V. Stein, Le vice-consul*, "Aurélia Steiner," and *L'amant*, to mention only the texts that I am particularly concerned with in this study.

In *La douleur* (meanings for the word are "pain," "sorrow," "grief"), we learn how intimately Duras was involved with world history in those early years. We learn that her first husband (Robert Antelme), a member of the Resistance, was returned to her from Dachau at the point of death, weighing eighty-four pounds (at five feet ten inches tall); that she nursed him away from death, one teaspoon of gruel at a time. We learn that she was in the Resistance; that François Morland, *nom de guerre* of François Mitterand, arranged to get Antelme out; that she participated in the interrogation and beating of a collaborator; and that she felt an attraction for a young and handsome member of the militia, a collaborator, whom she and her compatriots in the Resistance were detaining after the liberation.

In a brief preamble to two of the texts in the memoir, Duras writes: "Je vous donne celle qui torture avec le reste des textes. Apprenez à lire: ce sont des textes sacrés" (*LD* 134). (I give you she who tortures along with the rest of the texts. Learn to read: these texts are sacred.) During the time Duras herself had forgotten them, before it was known that they existed, could these early texts have been discovered, found out—read—*in* her later writings? Now, by the light of *La douleur*, that history, how will those stories be read? The line between recollection and invention expands or contracts depending on the text, but the two seemingly contradictory remarks Duras has made about this memoir—that *La douleur* is not "writing" and that these texts are sacred—raise more questions than they give answers. Questions of representation are embedded in these enigmatic and cryptic statements. Perhaps answers to what is representable, what can be read or what can be called writing, are glimpsed only in the circulation of more texts—story and history.

Duras experiments not only with the blanks in the chain, as she put it, but with the forms of her work. It is not always easy to tell the difference between her plays, screenplays, and novels. The full title for her scenario, *India Song*, for example, is *India Song: Texte, théâtre, film.* There is a sense of indeterminacy in her work. Her texts are fluid, full of movement but not plot. Nothing much happens in them. It is not always clear who is speaking, who has anything reliable to say. In her narratives, there is usually a "third," someone who watches the scene; often there is someone who writes: Aurélia Steiner, Jack Hold (*Le ravissement*),[8] Peter Morgan (*Le vice-consul*). The subject slips and slides, often floats, through the narratives, and there is very little ground for anyone, especially the reader, to hang on to. Writing worlds within her words, on the one hand, and making her subject disappear, on the other, Duras is a figure of both modernism and postmodernism.

In a body of work that is often said to be about the passions and madness of love and desire, Duras writes about what is at the limit, at the edge; about the thinnest of lines that falls between love and violence, between passion and madness; and about death, the inescapable shadow of desire—the end of desire. In that abyss of between is world history. It is there in her words, *ces trous,* her written spaces. Such is her scene of writing.

Francis Bacon took the title of Montaigne's *Essais* to mean "dispersed meditations,"[9] a perception that can, in my view, be a way of thinking about writing and of writing about writing that is innovative and fruitful and that problematizes customary formal and generic bases. The notion of dispersed meditations allows the disparate works of Arendt, Drabble, and Duras to be juxtaposed in such a study as the one I have undertaken here. The differences between the types of writing have not been eliminated by this approach. Such a problematization functions diacritically to reveal their nuances, their differences in detail, that their subsumption into conventional categories tends to wash out, reducing them to type.

Although Arendt is involved in writing political theory, she is not beyond language and literary concerns and matters of experience. Although Drabble writes about the experiences of women in apparently conventional forms and language, she is also writing unconventional meditations about how women *and* men live in an indeterminate and inhospitable world. And although Duras writes experimental fiction, stories of love between men and women that she hardly tells, she is inscribing that love in a written past of unspeakable, unrepresentable violations—her way of thinking about a past sempiternally forgotten, remembered, returned. The work of these writers is different from that of many other writers, women in particular, because it contains no privileged designs, no ends in sight, no utopias waiting. These writers attempt to show the world and the work as unfinished and that there is no "telling it like it is," because the telling is subject to the tyrannies of the telling itself. The representation of experience is always already subjected to language itself (which inescapably consititutes and is constituted by civilization) and cannot be "unwritten" to be rewritten "correctly."

No synthesis can be made of the work of Drabble, Duras, and Arendt, no closure. Each must be considered discretely, in their particularity, despite the connections I have made among them. I draw no conclusions that I have not already drawn in each chapter, so there is no chapter named "Conclusion" in my text. I leave it poised on a horizon of possibilities. It is open-ended, beckoning more essays, experiments, and experiences to be written, of which there can be only effects: meaning and some recognition. Above all, there is no pot of truth whose coin we should all like to pocket waiting at the end of the rainbow. It has been too late for that for a very long time, especially since World War II. Of open endings, Gertrude Stein wrote in *The Geographical History of America,* "Oblige me by not beginning. Also by not ending" (193). Though I did begin, I oblige by not ending. I remain in the in-between.

Chapter 2

Margaret Drabble

Nor will he [the cultured and fascinating liar] be welcomed by society alone. Art, breaking from the prison-house of realism, will run to greet him, and will kiss his false, beautiful lips, knowing that he alone is in possession of the great secret of all her manifestations, the secret that Truth is entirely and absolutely a matter of style.

—Oscar Wilde, "The Decay of Lying"

Lies, lies, it's all lies. A pack of lies. I've even told lies of fact, which I had not meant to do. Oh, I meant to deceive, I meant to draw analogies, but I've done worse than that, I've misrepresented.

—Margaret Drabble, *The Waterfall*

The fantasy . . . is to hear something else.

—Roland Barthes

Although in *The Waterfall* the narrator-protagonist Jane Gray extolls honesty and clarity in writing, she still claims that the story she just told about herself and her lover, James, is not the truth. She has not deliberately lied, yet she has been dishonest. She is guilty of omission. Reflecting on this, she writes:

I have often thought . . . that the ways of regarding an event so different don't add up to a whole; they are mutually exclusive: the social view, the circumstantial view, the moral view, these visions contradict each other; they do not supplement one another, they cancel one another, they destroy one another. They cannot co-exist. (*W* 47)

The whole story cannot be told. With each view there is another story, a different story, each one silences the other, and no one of them is truer than any other—perhaps none of them is true. These are not fragmented views that originated in some prior whole, nor will they one day, with the right combination of words or with an added measure of astuteness, be synthesized into a better, stronger whole.

Jane affirms the world as she perceives it: "But the air [in which love lives] is the real air, I know it. I can't make the connections; I can't join it up. And yet love has a reality, a quotidian reality, it must have, everything has" (*W* 90). She perceives the world as precarious and filled with the "mysteriousness of the usual." For instance, the random and, in the main, banal reasons she gives for falling in love with James include that he drove too fast, he was kind to his child, and she saw his "naked wrists against a striped tea towel once, seven years ago" (*W* 70). She accepts chance (examples of which abound in Drabble's work)[1] and refuses valuation. Indeterminacy is a guiding principle.[2]

Rather than represent the world mimetically in language while remaining indifferent and invisible, Drabble relinquishes that authorial stance and interrogates the world and herself in the process[3]—invents them as she writes her story. Michel Butor's remarks about writers and readers are apposite: "S'il est capable d'inventer, il pourra s'approcher de ce qui fut. Imaginer la réalité même" (Butor, "La Critique" 14). (If he [the reader] is capable of inventing, he will be able to approach what actually was—to imagine reality itself.) Any attempt to reconstruct a life (story) must necessarily result in fiction. In Jane's words:

> I must make an effort to comprehend it [life]. I will take it all to pieces, I will resolve it to its parts, and then I will put it together again, I will reconstitute it in a form that I can accept, a fictitious form: adding a little here, abstracting a little there, moving this arm half an inch that way, gently altering the dead angle of the head upon its neck. If I need a new morality, I will create one: a new ladder, a new virtue. If I need to understand what I am doing, if I cannot act without my own approbation—and I must act, I have changed, I am no longer capable of inaction—then I will invent a morality that condones me. Though by doing so, I risk condemning all that I have been. (*W* 53–54)

Reconstitution here is not resolution or synthesis but invention that renders the work and the world as incomplete. Butor, who sees criticism and invention as two aspects of the same activity, writes: "L'activité critique consiste à considerer les oeuvres comme inachevées, l'activité poetique, 'l'inspiration' manifeste la réalité même comme inachevée" (Butor, "La Critique" 20). (The critical activity consists in considering works as incomplete, the poetic activity, the "inspiration," manifests reality itself as unfinished.)

Jane discusses the ending of her story. Of the auto accident in which James was badly injured and she and her children were unscathed, she writes:

> There isn't any conclusion. A death would have been the answer, but nobody died. Perhaps I should have killed James in the car, and that would have made a neat, a possible ending.
>
>   A feminine ending?
>
>   Or, I could have maimed James so badly, in this narrative, that I would have been allowed to have him, as Jane Eyre had her blinded Rochester. (*W* 248)

Between death and disability, two possible endings for her story, Jane inserts a three-word paragraph—a noun phrase—that lacks a verb and ends with a question mark. The phrase seems ambiguous. Does it modify the previous sentence? If so, why consign the phrase, a tiny sentence fragment, to a new paragraph of its own? It does not modify the following sentence either, by virtue of the deftly placed "or" at the beginning of that sentence (and paragraph). I suggest that there is no ambiguity here at all. A feminine ending is precisely what Jane has given her story.

A technical term of prosody with which Jane is undoubtedly familiar because she is a practicing and published poet, a feminine ending, according to the *Princeton Encyclopedia of Poetry and Poetics,* "has the last stress on the penultimate (or even antepenultimate) syllable and most often requires terminal extrametrical syllables." James's recovery from the accident has the stress or the strong accent in the final pages of the novel, but that is not the end. There is an addendum to the story (an account of a weekend in Yorkshire during which James and Jane see "the celebrated waterfall") and a postscript—in prosodic terms, two extra syllables after the last stress—a classic feminine ending, indeed. Had Jane chosen to have James die, her ending, to pursue the prosodic analogy, would have been masculine, the final stress on the last syllable. It would have been, moreover, an end-stopped line (characteristic of the heroic couplet popular in eighteenth-century English poetry) in which both the meaning and the meter stop at the end of the line and death is, most literally, the end of the line—the last stop.

The sense of an ongoing ending is underscored by the note of uncertainty with which the last sentence leaves us: "I prefer to suffer, *I think*" (*W* 256; my emphasis). Nothing is sure in life except death, which one staves off with love (or in more current parlance, desire). To paraphrase Rilke, a woman gives birth to two fruits: a child and death (23). Life in all its harsh indeterminacy is to be suffered—and most acutely by women. But they need not capitulate or resign themselves to what feminist critic Elaine Showalter, speaking of Drabble's heroines, has called a "feminine destiny" or the "curse of Eve" (*A Literature of Their Own* 307).

Suffering is generally construed to be a form of passivity. It is easy enough to equate passivity with femininity, and activity with masculinity. These are commonplace cultural connections. We could conclude, then, that Jane's preference for suffering is a feminine ending—weak, even masochistic. Freud, in his essay "Femininity," warns against such facile equations and conclusions.

> It seems to me to serve no useful purpose and adds nothing to our knowledge. One might consider characterizing femininity psychologically as giving preference to passive aims. This is not, of course, the same thing as passivity; to achieve a passive aim may call for a large amount of activity. (102)

Having a thrombic clot in her leg—"the price that modern women pay for love" (*W* 256)—Jane has to stop taking birth control pills. Musing over this turn of events, she writes the last lines of the book.

> In the past, in old novels, the price of love was death, a price which virtuous women paid in childbirth and the wicked, like Nana, with the pox. Nowadays it is paid in thrombosis or neurosis: one can take one's pick. I stopped taking those pills, as James lay there unconscious and motionless, but one does not escape decision so easily. I am glad of this. I am glad I cannot swallow pills with immunity. I prefer to suffer, I think. (*W* 256)

Suffering is etymologically linked to patience and passion. Among the meanings for *passion* are "intense, driving, overmastering feeling"; "an outbreak of anger"; "ardent affection"; and "love and sexual desire."

Jane's decision to struggle with the precariousness of life bespeaks activity, not passivity. Those last words, "I think," bring to mind Descartes's cogito (historically, thinking has rarely been considered a feminine attribute) corrupted and parodied: I suffer therefore I am (I think); I think (I am) therefore I suffer. Either way activity prevails. Yet the ending of the book is feminine prosodically speaking.

"A feminine ending?" the noun phrase with a question mark that is its own paragraph, is the ambiguous (and ironic) pivot on which all these relations of sexual difference are hinged. Jane has been able to present them in an enriching complexity because she has delivered them in literary terms. She does not, like Anna Wulf, Doris Lessing's writer-protagonist in *The Golden Notebook,* try to capture reality in a series of notebooks. Instead she invents it by telling her story and thus reveals it obliquely. Rather than choose the authority of experience like Lessing, Drabble experiments like Gertrude Stein. Because the name Gertrude Stein is virtually synonymous with experimental writing, a brief digression into some aspects of her work may serve to situate Drabble in a new context that may unmoor her from the position she has been given as a novelist of women's experience.

It remains a great irony that not any of her most audacious works but one overtly more conventional first brought Gertrude Stein international fame. The book, however, is a deception. Worse than that, to recall Drabble's admission, it is a misrepresentation. Called *The Autobiography of Alice B. Toklas,* it was written by Gertrude Stein. The title page of the Harcourt first edition makes no mention of Stein's authorship. The editor, it appears, was in collusion with the author to keep the reader from learning that the book is not what the title says it is—until the last page, where Stein as Toklas writes:

> About six weeks ago Gertrude Stein said, it does not look to me as if you are going to write that autobiography. You know what I am going to do. I am going to write it simply as Defoe did the autobiography of Robinson Crusoe. And she has and this is it. (310)

Stein's reference to Defoe's work is more than just "mischievous fun," as Elizabeth Sprigge, one of her biographers puts it (172). It is a subversion of the genre. Defoe wrote an extremely detailed account of the life of Robinson Crusoe, of which he says in his preface, "The editor believes the thing to be a just history of fact; neither is there any appearance of fiction in it." The fact is, however, that *Robinson Crusoe* is fictitious, and so is Toklas's autobiography.

With its last words, *The Autobiography of Alice B. Toklas* erases itself and is replaced by the autobiography of Gertrude Stein, in which Stein is both the narrator and the main character, invariably called Gertrude Stein. Who, then, is Alice B. Toklas? In *The Autobiography*, she is fictitious; she exists as Stein's fiction by virtue of a generic title that belies its contents. The book allows just one innocent reading, that can take place only if the reader has not heard of its famous ruse. Prior knowledge (of the deception) turns every reading into a rereading that can never be accomplished without a splitting of the reader's consciousness: "I know very well who the author is, but all the same . . . " The identity of the narrator, the character Gertrude Stein, and the author Stein, is forever problematized, as is the notion of an ending (of a work). The last paragraph of *The Autobiography* may be a joke on the reader, but it is also an invitation to a rereading. It is tantamount to an ending marked da capo, and thus it is the sense of the beginning jarred: one does not begin, one begins again—the same follows, but differently. "Oblige me by not beginning. Also by not ending," writes Gertrude Stein (*Geographical History* 193).

Because *The Autobiography* has no "true" beginning or ending, and because the identities of the principals—indeed of the very self of the title—are in question (to say nothing of complaints of "falsities" by many of the painters and writers whom Stein portrayed in the book [Sprigge 199]), reference to Defoe, master of the appearance of truth and so a liar nonpareil, is a brilliant stroke of literary allusion—a masterstroke, nay, a "materstroke," to mimic Stein's telling wordplay in the following lines from her *Geographical History*.

> In knowing everything never being left alone there makes a recognition of what mater-pieces are.
> Knowing everything is never left alone nor is it ever without being knowing everything. Anything else is of no account. Not in mater-pieces. (232)

Stein's omission of the *s* in masterpieces is intriguing, especially because it is the only instance in the book of such an irregularity. Is it an error? Or just an oversight? A slip? Or another joke? Whichever it is, something—as we have learned from Freud, for whom such lapses were manifestations of the unconscious—has gotten by the psychic censor.

The word *mater-pieces* has a distinctly feminine cast, which is perfectly fitting because Stein says in *Geographical History* that "a woman in this epoch does the important literary thinking" (220). That woman is her: "So then the important literary thinking is being done. / Who does it. / I do it. / Oh yes I do it" (222). The feminizing here not only takes place in the substitution of *mater* for *master* but lies in a kind of shock that the word *masterpieces* receives. Without the *s,* the word is pried loose from its moorings, the notions of closure and fixity that reside in it are shaken up. The missing *s* thus gives the word some play, puts it into play—and Gertrude Stein, it is well known, took her wordplay very seriously.

As Alice Jardine says in an essay on feminism and writing, "the woman who finds the courage to write in patriarchal culture . . . must use every ounce of her wit(s)" ("Pre-Texts" 230). A *witz* or a joke is a jest that "possesses substance and value," wrote Freud in *Jokes and their Relation to the Unconscious* (131). The exercise of play, the instability and uncertainty in/of language (and its significations and referents), has been said to be a feminization of writing (See Derrida, *Spurs*). Such an exercising of language, instead of obscuring meaning, opens the way to a multiplicity of meanings, an overdetermination (Freud, *Interpretation of Dreams* 182, 253, 341–43) of literary material that cannot be exhausted by one essential meaning or truth.

Drabble's feminine ending is reminiscent of Stein's da capo in *The Autobiography of Alice B. Toklas*—unstressed and ongoing. Like *The Autobiography, The Waterfall* is not obviously but deceptively experimental. Both writers make a show of telling the truth: Stein by falsely calling her book an autobiography (the genre of confession), Drabble by having her writer-narrator persistently question the truth of her own story. In both works, the third-person protagonist and the narrator are the same person: Drabble has Jane step in and out of her role as the *she* in the story and the *I* in her simultaneous narrative about the story; Stein creates herself as her third person and invents Alice B. Toklas as her *I*. These first and third persons are conventions of the writing and are fictitious. With genres subverted and convention sabotaged, how does truth emerge?—as a matter of style, to recall my Wilde epigraph.

Although she has been highly praised, Drabble has not been read as though she were a contemporary stylist. According to Michael F. Harper, in an illuminating essay on her work, "Margaret Drabble is widely seen as a late twentieth-century novelist who writes what many reviewers have taken to be good, solid nineteenth-century novels." She is spoken of as having "pure, old-fashioned narrative skill" and as writing "solid pieces of realistic fiction" (Harper 148–49).[4] She has at times even corroborated these assessments, but Harper gives some trenchant reasons for this in his essay, which makes a strong case for the contemporaneity of Drabble's work. With the exception of Harper's essay, readings of Drabble have been naive. She has been read at face value, with little apprehension of the irony that pervades her form and language.

Gayatri Spivak, though not reading Drabble naively in the same way other feminist critics do, does give her a reductive reading. In her essay "Three Feminist Readings: McCullers, Drabble, Habermas," Spivak claims that Jane has indulged in an "orthodox privileging of the aesthetic," to "resolve and reconstitute life"—typical of the "humanist academic" (24–29). The point of my reading, quite to the contrary, is that for Drabble there is no resolution or reconstitution, even in fiction that is not a misrepresentation, a deceit. Spivak does not actually deny this but condemns Drabble for her ironic and paradoxical language and novelistic strategies as classbound and unregeneratively privatistic, as thwarted in her seriousness as a writer. In the service of a taxonomic (categories of race, class, and sex that must be addressed by serious feminist writers) rather than an exclusivist practice as a criterion of literary value (i.e., "If she is a feminist, she must try to change the world"), Spivak admits, *"I am projecting an ideal whole* [my emphasis] that subsumes novels and social problematics *and* our own lives as fragmented texts" (29). This, I contend, (as does Harper) is precisely what Drabble rejects. There is no longer "an ideal whole"; there are only, in Virginia Woolf's words, "scraps, orts, and fragments" (*Between the Acts* 189). Although Spivak states that she (Spivak) is engaged in "intertextuality," the "weaving in texts of 'book,' 'world,' and 'life'" (29), I argue that she is doing the opposite, that is, making a case under other guises for the representation of "real" life in art whose aims are utopic or instructive at least.

Showalter's reading of Drabble (though different from Spivak's) is particularly reductive. She labels her "a novelist of maternity," because her novels are usually concerned, to one degree or another, with motherhood (*A Literature of Their Own* 305). *The Waterfall* deals to some extent with childbirth—but not in any ordinary or predictable way. The love affair between Jane and James begins immediately after Jane, separated from her husband, Malcolm, has delivered her second child, alone, with the aid of a midwife. James and his wife, Lucy (Jane's first cousin), come daily to stay with Jane as she recovers. After a few days, James returns alone and sits by her bed—in the delivery room, as it were—and tends to her. They fall in love. James implores her to allow him to sleep with her chastely in the warmth of the birthing bed while her body heals. In a most erotic love scene in which there is no sexual encounter, no embrace or kiss, Drabble has managed with consummate skill to depict a woman as she is rarely shown—as, at once, sexually desirable and a mother figure. With the same stroke, she has also depicted a man's unending desire for his mother (for a return to that "desperate paradise" [Mehlman, *Structural Study of Autobiography* 25], that lost oneness he knew with her in his earliest months) and for his lover who is the substitute for the mother. Because between them there has been no sex in this bed, only the recent birth, it is as though James were pretending it was he who was born. With Jane's husband absent, James is also pretender to her love and the male position in her life. When a midwife, on her evening rounds, calls James "Mr. Gray," he does not correct her (*W* 21).

The story of James, the Old Pretender (James, Francis Edward Stuart), who was called James III of Scotland and James VIII of England, is one of illegitimacy, not only in matters of royal succession, or of paternity, which is never sure, but, startlingly, of maternity as well. History has it that "at his birth it was widely believed that he was an imposter who was slipped into the Queen's bed in a warming pan in order to provide a Catholic successor to the throne."[5] The resonance is unmistakable: James slips into Jane Gray's bed whose namesake, Lady Jane Gray, was indeed queen of England, but only for nine days (another pretender). When William of Orange deposed James II, the infant prince was taken to France, where a court in exile had been set up. When James II died, Louis XIV proclaimed James king of England.

James Otford and Jane Gray, with her two children, set up a kind of ménage, outside the law, alongside their legitimate ones—his with Lucy and hers, legally at least, with Malcolm. (The historical Malcolm is a legitimate king of Scotland, son of Duncan, whose murder by Macbeth is immortalized in Shakespeare's play.) When catastrophe strikes, Jane becomes a pretender vis-à-vis her cousin Lucy, to whom she bears a strong resemblance. At the time of the accident, Jane is taken for Mrs. Otford, a mistaken identity that Lucy, for the sake of propriety and efficiency, must comply with and even compound by briefly assuming Jane's name. Lucy telephones Jane at the hotel near the hospital to which James was taken. Jane writes:

> The pageboy came and said to me that Mrs. Jane Gray was asking for me on the telephone. I had such a shock at the sound of my own name that I could hardly stand up: it seemed all too absurd, like some dreadful Elizabethan comedy of impersonation and mistaken identity. (*W* 223)

When Lucy arrives at the hotel, she must book her room in Jane's name and address because Jane is already registered as Mrs. James Otford (pretenders abound).

Jane's illegitimate position is so much on her mind that when she receives a letter from Malcolm's lawyer informing her of his intention to sue for divorce, naming James, she thinks of Jane Gray with her head on the block (*W* 242). Lady Jane Gray, the great-granddaughter of Henry VII, was beautiful and intelligent, had excellent tutors, and spoke and wrote Latin and Greek at an early age. Her father-in-law, duke of Northumberland, persuaded dying Edward VI to designate Lady Jane successor to the throne, bypassing her cousins, princesses Mary and Elizabeth, daughters of her uncle (her mother's brother) Henry VIII. Some months after her nine-day reign at the age of sixteen, Lady Jane was arrested and beheaded.[6]

Drabble, at home in a company of pretenders, is herself a pretender par excellence who admits it. Recall, for example, the lines from the epigraph in which she and Jane signal the reader to be wary: "Oh, I *meant* to deceive, I *meant* to draw analogies, but I've done worse than that, I've *misrepresented*" (my emphasis). Not only is *The Waterfall* a double-tracked narrative of story and commentary, but the work itself can be read on two tracks of meaning. On one, the book works admirably as a sophisticated love story, a modern tale of adultery. On the other, it is a highly wrought parody of the English tradition—that is, English history and literature woven into the textuality that is that tradition.

The literariness of *The Waterfall* renders the novel a "mater-piece" of irony. Everywhere there is usually something more than meets the eye. Exceptionally "materful" about *The Waterfall* is that its irony is quietly subversive, deeply embedded in the surface. No other, "real" meaning is hidden beneath a false or shallow surface meaning. The surface—Drabble's art—reveals itself to whatever extent it can be read. The novel is full of jokes, snares, and lies. Some take the form of obvious literary allusions. Jane Gray frequently refers to Jane Eyre (both the book and the character) and so gives the impression that Eyre is her literary ancestor rather than Lady Jane Grey. Drabble's Jane is parodying Jane Eyre as a literary prototype for smart but neurotic heroines (usually English) of the literary persuasion—like herself.

In the paragraph that begins, "Lies, lies, it's all lies. A pack of lies . . . ," Jane, trying to describe her passion for James, says in a final burst, "Reader, I loved him: as Charlotte Brontë said"—and she tells yet another lie or two (*W* 89). Neither Brontë nor Jane Eyre made this particular statement. The line alluded to is Jane Eyre's, and it is actually, "Reader, I married him" (452)—a vast difference in emphasis, among other things, that bespeaks the difference between the two works. Jane and James never marry, but they continue their love affair. In addition, the rather contemptuous reference Jane Gray makes to the maiming (of Rochester) is necessary to Brontë's story but not to hers (*W* 248).

Drabble's onomastic art demonstrates the power of the subversive and parodic wit that resides in her work. Using *Gray* as a spoiled anagram of *Eyre* is the means through which she has Jane let the reader know how absurd, yet how important, the concern with names, identity, and position is, when she describes her mother's anguish at having put the wrong middle initial on a letter to a titled parent of a student enrolled in the preparatory school her husband runs.

> I saw her grow pale, I saw the hours lengthen, I saw her bite her nails. I saw her panic, I saw her weep. For her error, for her crime. I saw her hair turn gray, for a G where there should have been an H. (*W* 61)

This observation, significant to the character of her mother, and perhaps to that of the English middle class, is also a comic moment—one of derision and satire from which the surnames of the two Janes are not exempt. Here the G takes the place of a possible *H* that a cockney pronunciation could give the name Eyre, the demonstration for which is given in the very sentence that describes the mistake: for "I saw her hair turn gray"—a play on words of outlandish proportions—read, "I saw her (Brontë's) Eyre turn (to) Gray." Drabble surely has her witz about her.

In case this wordplay is considered a fortuitous coincidence (and why not, since the play of language is often unconscious playing), I point to another instance of Drabble's ironic use of names, when James introduces Jane to the driver of his racing car.

> "My cousin Jane," he said, and Jane held out her hand to the man called Mike, and he took it. . . . On the back of his hand he had a tatoo, which said:
>
>
>
> B
>
> B O B
>
> B
>
>
>
> and she very much approved of the poetic symmetry of this declaration. (*W* 79)

That the name is a palindrome that can be read vertically as well as horizontally, creating a kind of *calligramme*—the figure of the cross—underscores the joke on the logos and herself: "Ah, love" (*W* 62).

Furthermore, Drabble is presenting us with a notion of meaning that is produced in a relation of difference in which identity does not exist. The difference in the names of James and Jane is as big and as small as the difference between the *m* and the *n*, the two consecutive letters of the alphabet that appear in their one-syllable names; the *s* in James is left over. The serpentine, insinuating *s* is the letter in English of possession—which is highly ironic because there is very little that James can claim as his own—and of plurality—the stigma of irony, more than one meaning.

A large part of the subversive and the parodic in Drabble consists in a rich comic thread present in all her novels, an example of which is the motif of teeth that runs through *The Realms of Gold*. Teeth and bones are what is left for survivors and archeologists (of whom the protagonist, Frances Wingate, is one). Not only are there toothaches, extractions, and emergency visits to dentists in foreign countries in the book, but Frances, briefly separated from her lover, carries with her everywhere his false teeth (a removable bridge), keeps them in a drawer near her bed (along with his letters), wherever she is. She had taken also to wearing them in the front of her brassiere.

She liked the feel of them, Karel's teeth resting gently and delicately and wirily against her soft evening breast, they kept her company. She had one low-cut dress that she was rather fond of, a soft black one, soft black wool, and one night at a party she caught a man in the act of staring down her cleavage and meeting, entranced and horrified, the sight of Karel's glaring teeth, the guardians of her virtue. She had taken a man back home with her from that party, an old colleague and friend, and as they got undressed for bed, she got out the teeth and put them on the bedside table, and John had stared at them in alarm, and she told him what and whose they were, and they had lain in each other's arms all night, quietly, watched over by those luminous dentures, gleaming pale like ivory, more vigilant than a nun's candle. . . . A little of Karel's virtue had breathed its way through even so poor a relic.

She and Karel had planned, once, to visit Pilsen, but they hadn't made it. He had not been there since he was a small child. Most of his family had perished in concentration camps. He alone of his generation escaped. Teeth and bones. Profanely she cherished his fragments. (*RG* 20)

This passage borders on the grotesque. Much of its humor comes from the unexpected, from the juxtaposition of the profane and the sacred, and in the last paragraph, from a metonymic connection between false teeth as relic, and teeth and bones as remains. Except for Karel and his aunt, only ashes—and perhaps the gold teeth and fillings—were left of Karel's family (and of those millions of others) due to the relentless Nazi crematoria. And "his fragments" are false teeth, a prosthesis, his/not his, like writing in relation to experience, to life.

When the flashback is over, Drabble brings us back to the novel's present very early in the book, to a restaurant in North Africa where Frances has just arrived for an archeologists' meeting. The recollection has kindled her desire to have the teeth right then. Trying to visualize where in her luggage they might be, she thinks: "She had taken them to Turin, hadn't she, on that last trip. Or had she?" (*RG* 20). Ending the entire sequence by offhandedly mentioning the place known for the most celebrated of relics is to compare Frances's couple of false teeth to the Shroud of Turin, a final odd and funny touch. As Drabble writes in *The Middle Ground,* "life is too bizarre for fiction, these days" (174). The teeth turn up here and there throughout the novel, and at the end, they hang on the doorknob of a hotel wardrobe during a visit to Prague, in which Karel weeps into Frances's shoulder because of the solitary and impoverished condition of his aged aunt, the only one left in Europe of all his family. The incongruity of the teeth hanging there amidst Karel's weeping and Frances's thoughts of death and "dust and ashes rising from a crematorium chimney . . . , the gold baroque of Prague, and Kafka the mad Jew and those perilous grave stones" (*RG* 322) lifts the implacable sadness of survival, of life itself, for just a moment or two and lets in a spot of joy, clears a space for some serious thinking and for a bit of rejoicing. One comic image permits a thousand serious and unbearable thoughts—teeth as protector gods, indeed.

The Needle's Eye also contains a comic vein, a leitmotiv pronounced by the book's title, that of being too rich to enter the kingdom of heaven. Rose Vassilou tries to divest herself of her inheritance, but they are not easily parted. Considered highly eccentric, Rose suffers, trying to live up to the standards of her conscience, the effects on her psyche of a too early exposure to scripture by an overly zealous and repressive nanny, Noreen (the negative cast to her name is glaring). Although the overall effect of Noreen on Rose is serious, the unfolding and recounting of the various consequences of her tutelage are comic and ironic. The irony cuts both ways: though funny, it is nonetheless sad and serious. This humor should not be missed or misread as most feminists (and other critics) often do. It is a vein of very dark comedy—in some places, black.

The play in Drabble's language is aural and visible. Names are the fairest of game, and none is exempt. In some cases the play is obvious. For instance, Gabriel Denham wears denim clothes and gets his name misspelled frequently: "I keep getting letters addressed to Mr. Denim these days" (*MG* 221). In other instances the play is subtler. In *The Realms of Gold,* Frances Wingate's eccentric old aunt, Constance Ollerenshaw, scandalized the family by dying alone of starvation and not being found until she was in the last stages of decay. She was a romantic figure, who as a result of an adulterous love affair suffered great losses: her illegitimate child died at eighteen months, and her lover three years later. After a stay at a nursing home, she lived a solitary, reclusive, and long life. Constance is called Aunt Con most of the time, and her lover, thinks Frances, reading his letters to her aunt, might have been, among other things, "a con man" (*RG* 279). The connection Constance/Con is an antonymy, an unsettling onomastic equivocation on the notion of constancy that casts a shadow on Drabble's seemingly sunny ending to *The*

Realms of Gold—all live happily ever after, spending summers and holidays in Aunt Con's (refurbished) cottage—and that suggests Drabble's invitation to the reader to "invent a more suitable ending if you can" (*RG* 324).

Margaret Homans sees the character of the aunt as a "feminine intrusion" (feminine because, according to Homans's feminist reasoning, Con was not—as Frances is—assimilated into the [masculine] world). She sees her as a "feminine intrusion" that Drabble suppresses "in order to have the story close happily" ("Her Very Own Howl" 204). Because Homans does not take the name into account, does not read it, she loses the cutting edge of Con's place in the novel. Aunt Con is the patron saint of fiction, of the story itself, of the "set-up," and the premier con artist is Drabble. There *is* a feminine intrusion, to use Homans's locution, but on other grounds. *Con* is French slang for dumb, stupid, a word equivalent to the English *cunt*. It is evident from Drabble's work that her French is good enough for her to be aware of this. There is a certain *con*centricity[7] (as opposed to phallocentricity), a certain woman-centeredness, about the aunt's nickname, in addition to the suggestion of cunning and deception. The con game, despite the fact that men play it all the time, is, it can be said, the woman's game. The Constance/Con opposition is filled with meaning that prevents the cover-up of which Homans accuses Drabble. The whole story (Is there a whole story?) of Con's tragic, wasted life may not be there, but far from being suppressed, she and her story are inscribed in the novel, in its very language, as a pivot between happy and sad, tragic and comic—a bit like life itself, untotalizable, open-ended. I think Drabble's happy ending is a con job, and those who believe it to be a happy ending have been conned.

Other names in Drabble's texts bear analysis. Language for Drabble is neither transparent nor reliable; rather, it discloses, to use a term of Arendt's. Her texts are surfaces on which the signifiers play, producing meaning. Often she simply has fun with words, plays with them without calling much attention to them (all emphasis in the following examples is mine): "Maria's *vest,* a hand-on, had huge holes under the armpits. 'Look at them, look at them,' said Emily, pausing on the steps, 'our little *vested* interests'" (*NE* 215); "They were all dead, all the young men and maidens, Antigone, *Hector,* Cressida, Orestes, Clytemnestra. . . . The Bursar's wife slept soundly in a warm damp bed gathering strength for the *hectoring* of the morrow" (*IA* 223); "Henrik, a historian . . . thought Wordsworth wasn't a *patch* on Goethe; they talked on of sex and poetry.

And Evelyn . . . wondered whether to get out her *patchwork*" (*MG* 213); "Out of date Marylou, clinking and shimmering like the old fashioned *solitaire* diamond on her finger. *Solitaire*. A *solitary* woman in a large house" (*MG* 199). Drabble reads signs, license plates, telegrams, and headlines that can be easily misread: "Through some peculiarity of the typography [of a sign on a hospital notice board], it appeared to read RENT-A-RAT instead of RENT-A-FLAT" (*MG* 135). In *The Ice Age,* Stan had an "urgent desire to purchase a car number plate . . . . SO SEXY, it said, though one could see on close inspection that it read in fact 50 5EXY" (*MG* 53).

For Drabble (as for Stein), the letter speaks; it is a touchstone of meaning. In *The Needle's Eye,* she has Simon Camish say in a conversation at a party:

> The law . . . as an institution, is admirable, they've got it all wrong, it's the uses to which it is put that are all wrong. It isn't the letter that kills and the spirit that giveth life at all, it's the other way round. The spirit kills and the letter gives life. (257)

The resonance of Simon's remarks with a passage in a lecture of Lacan's called "The Agency of the Letter in the Unconscious or Reason since Freud," is inescapable. Lacan writes:

> Of course, as it is said, the letter killeth while the spirit giveth life. . . . But we should also like to know how the spirit could live without the letter. Even so, the pretensions of the spirit would remain unassailable if the letter had not shown us that it produces all the effects of truth in man without involving the spirit at all.
>
> It is none other than Freud who had this revelation, and he called his discovery the unconscious. (*Ecrits: A Selection* 158)

It is illuminating that so marked a connection can be found between the English Drabble, reputedly an old-fashioned and middlebrowed writer, and the French Lacan, a controversial and difficult thinker important in current theoretical explorations in literature and psychoanalysis. The connection is further indication that Drabble may be misconstrued, certainly mislabeled. The hinge on which this connection rests is the heart of the psychoanalytic discovery: the unconscious, which renders the subject decentered, dispersed, that is, irrevocably split and constituted in language. The virility of the lettered unconscious is evident in Drabble's work if the letters are read. Lacan, at the beginning of his lecture on "The Agency of the Letter in the Unconscious," asks, "But how are we to take this 'letter' here?" Answering his own question, he says, "Quite simply, literally" (à la lettre [Ecrits: A Selection 147]). But because what is literal is always already metaphorical and not the thing itself, the letter, the name, inscribes an approximation, a pretence, a displacement, and is thus overdetermined.

What then is the truth? Nietzsche writes that it is "a mobile army of metaphors, metonyms and anthropomorphisms—in short, a sum of human relations" ("On Truth and Lie" 46–47). The truth cannot be located, pinned down. It neither exists outside the text as experience nor is stashed away inside it like a treasure trove waiting to be discovered. It insists in the interminable chain of words that is the writing subject and is produced as an effect as it is read.

The relation between women's experience and literary experiment exists in just that, relation, as the two words *experience* and *experiment* themselves announce. The French word *expérience* means "experiment" in English, and in both languages, both words have the same etymology—from the Latin, formed on *experiri,* to try. I suggest that literary experiment is a means of trying on or trying out women's experience, of discovering it, of finding it (out); and interestingly enough, finding is another word for invention.

In *The Ice Age,* Drabble's placing of her beloved England in the path of an encroaching Pleistocene epoch is a preposterous fantasy—not as redundant a phrase as it may sound—in which what comes after now, the present, is not post or later but earlier. It is a previous (prehistoric) age as preposterous as *hysteron proteron,* which is the putting of the cart before the horse. It is like saying someone is "bred and born," not born again, although a little more faith in general is entirely consonant with Drabble's hope for England and her characters in this book. Some even say that there is a search for God, for religion, in it—an assertion for which there is certainly some evidence. A gloomy work in many ways, *The Ice Age* seems to hint at an impending doom that can be averted by the advent of an ice age—an apocalypse of sorts. The ice age, defined as "characterized by the alternate appearance and recession of northern glaciation,"[8] is a pervasive metaphor in the novel. It is a conceit, not of an end, but of a stoppage—a freeze frame—that slows things down just enough to reveal the possibility of a change of tone in the world. It also evokes Jacques Derrida's essay "Of an Apocalyptic Tone Recently Adopted in Philosophy," which he presented at a colloquium on his work called *Les Fins de l'homme* (*The Ends of Man*). To speak of the end(s) of man in proximity to the suggestion of an ice age, the epoch marked by the "appearance of the progenitor of man," is also preposterous, but not impossible.

The technical term for the ice age is the Pleistocene epoch, from the Greek *pleistos* (most) and *kainos* (new or recent). It comes before the Holocene or the present epoch and after the Pliocene. Its name and place are designations of the geological time scale, an abstraction that is usually shown as a column of rock sequences divided into spaces named eras, periods, and epochs—terms, in descending order of inclusivity, that indicate time spans. The Pleistocene epoch is both the newest division of the Pliocene epoch and the older division of the post-Tertiary period. Like Duchamp's door that closes one space while opening another, the ice age is both old and new: it is the closing and opening of a space of time.

Like the ice age, Drabble the writer sits between the old, the great Victorian age of English novel writing, and the new, newer than the recent modernist period, the contemporary experimental work that has come to be called postmodern (from the Latin *post* plus *modo,* "after now"). The name attached to this time frame of a space of writing is an emblem of the preposterous. What is beyond the new, past the now, is a future condition that is unrepresentable unless based on some version of an already existing reality, because the inherent condition of representation is its pastness. The postmodern points to the future as it suggests the past. As Jean-François Lyotard writes, "the postmodern is the modern, not at its end but in its nascent state" (*Postmodern Condition* 79). It is a beforehand given in an afterward—bred and born.

The sense of the postmodern is one of contingency. It can best be expressed by the future perfect tense: what *will have been done* once the duration of a work has ended. For example, this or that account of an experience will have been a story, a history, a novel; or, he or she (a character in a work) will have been through hell. The future perfect suggests a doing, a making—not what has happened, but what has been made to happen by the writing. The tense can be viewed as straddling both the indicative and the subjunctive moods, because an object is made (e.g., a novel), but its existence is contingent on its being played out in a duration in which the future and its past meet. The postmodern is a consideration of what is presentable, of what can be written when the epistemologies that constitute our notion of representation are changing—have indeed changed. Plots and characters in many postmodern works are no longer shackled to a conventional psychology and couched in a univalent language. The postmodern is a criticism (emphasizing here its relation to *crisis*) of representation, of, more inclusively, writing itself. Drabble articulates this postmodern condition with a writing style comprised, as I have demonstrated above, of a finely distilled English literary prose laced with a sharply honed wit (a venerable part of the English tradition) and an irony that cuts a double track of meaning. What you see is *not* all you get, but what is seen is highly readable (or misreadable), regardless of the track.

It is appropriate to say here, *Caveat lector!* A reader proceeds in Drabble at his or her own risk. There are few certainties, and the verities are rocky (a truly ambiguous word). Time and the order of things are not monoliths but malleable concepts. In Drabble's lexicon, time is a chronology that is as arbitrary as any other sequence, the alphabet for one. She puts it this way when she gives us one of the meditations Alison Murray (who lives with Anthony Keating, the protagonist) has in *The Ice Age*.

> Time, she came to think, is not consequential: it occurs simultaneously, and distributed through it in meaningless chronology are spots of sorrow, spots of joy. We combine them as we will, as we can best bear them. We make our own ordering. (247)

Sometimes we do so preposterously, that is, illogically, absurdly. Absurdity is very much a part of the postmodern spectrum.

There is a certain shiftiness about things chez Drabble—High Rook House, Anthony's seventeenth-century country home north of England, the locale for much of *The Ice Age*. The house is named for the rooks that nest in a huge old elm in the lane. A rook is a raucous-voiced black bird resembling a carrion crow, whose species ranges discontinuously from England to Iran and Manchuria, and the word *rook* can be applied to persons as an abusive and disparaging term. Warnings and intimations of the comic, or worse, of a scam, of traps being laid, are not too far afield. The book is about the wheelings and dealings that take place in the worlds of real estate and high finance, where high rookery is not unknown. A rook after all is a crook who can cover a lot of ground: the one piece in the chess game that can move forward and backward and across the board. Drabble is a bird of such a feather.

There are all manner of birds in *The Ice Age*. It begins and ends with a bird. More accurately, it begins with more than one bird, because the novel begins before its beginning with its epigraphs, one of which speaks of birds. The epigraph, proemial in nature, stands astride a text, above it, attracting readers, offering them some direction, and (in this most like the proem) swaying them away from some other channel of entry. Drabble's first epigraph (the other is an excerpt from Wordsworth's poem written in 1802 calling Milton back to England again) is several lines from Milton's *Areopagitica*, written in 1644 on freedom of the English press. The significance of Milton in Drabble's text is cogently presented at some length by Ellen Cronan Rose in *The Novels of Margaret Drabble: Equivocal Figures*. As Rose points out, the spirit of Milton, the poet-philosopher—of the elegy *Lycidas*, which records his spiritual crisis at the accidental death of his friend, and of the epic *Paradise Lost*, which seeks to "justify the ways of God to Men" (what Anthony is determined to do at the end of the novel)—hovers over the book (118), but much more specifically, these particular lines from the *Areopagitica* insist in Drabble's text:

> Methinks I see in my mind a noble and puissant Nation rousing herself like a strong man after sleep, and shaking her invincible locks. Methinks I see her as an eagle muing her mighty youth, and kindling her undazl'd eyes at the full midday beam; purging and unscaling her long abused sight at the fountain itself of heavenly radiance; while the whole noise of timorous and flocking birds, with those also that love the twilight, flutter about, amaz'd at what she means, and in their envious gabble would prognosticate a year sects and schisms. (*IA* epigraph)

Rather than assuming the authoritarian, pedagogical distance that customarily accompanies notions of the epigraph, it might be more fruitful to think of this excerpt not in its epigraphical position but in a parasitical one in which Milton's lines play host to Drabble's text, as at a banquet—site and citation of intertextuality.

The concatenation of parasite, site, and citation in the last sentence brings to mind "The Critic as Host," a disquisition by J. Hillis Miller on the word *parasite* that presents its etymology and particularly the antithetical nature of the word (an idea central to my reading of this epigraph and the novel). *Parasite,* in its original meaning, according to Miller, "was something positive, a fellow guest, someone sharing the food with you, there with you beside the grain" (442). Appositely, Michel Serres writes in *The Parasite:* "The parasite is a thermal exciter. He aims to please at the *table d'hôte;* he is invited with this aim in mind. . . . Without him the feast is only a cold meal. His role is to animate the event" (190). Moreover, the host is not just an eater but what is eaten: he gives (of) himself in a partaking (of the host) that brings to mind the consecrated bread or wafer—the host of the Eucharist, and the host as victim, as sacrifice.

Are these connections between the epigraph and the text, and between Milton and Drabble, which have come about as a consequence of my reading, a matter of fate or just a lucky accident? They are a little of both perhaps—the very issues Drabble puts before us in *The Ice Age:* relations of chance, free choice, and necessity or fate. These issues have to do with the philosophical concerns of *Lycidas* and *Paradise Lost,* but Drabble's text is fed by the words Milton speaks in the *Areopagitica* about freedom in the marketplace (of ideas), in the public realm where the din and tumult make it difficult to hear and thus to see clearly. The effect of the excerpt is synesthetic: the light, the radiance in the mind's eye is dimmed by the noise of the "envious gabble" of the fluttering and flocking birds (coincidentally, in French the word *le parasite* also means static, noise).

The distance allowed by sight in the first half of the passage produces a great vision of nobility and power: "a strong man" and "shaking her *invincible* locks [my emphasis]" (the simile sparks some ambiguity of gender identification), and an eagle opening its eyes to the sun. This vision is held in check not only by the second half, where the vision is lost to sound, but by an ambiguity that exists in the word *muing*. The *Oxford English Dictionary* says that *muing* is "peculiarly used by Milton: [its] precise sense is difficult to determine." The meaning of the word is generally held to be "renewing" or "shedding" (the eagle as a symbol of renewal reinforces this, as does the notion of muing as the moulting of feathers). Embedded in the word also, however, is its antithesis: the notion of confining, of cooping or shutting up.

Freud realized the importance of psychiatrists knowing more about the development of language in general to understand the language of dreams. In his essay on "The Antithetical Sense of Primal Words," he reviews the work of philologist K. Abel on this subject and notes especially the following passage.

> "The essential relativity of all knowledge, thought, or consciousness cannot but show itself in language. If everything that we can know is viewed as a transition from something else, every experience must have two sides; and either every name must have a double meaning, or else for every meaning there must be two names." (60)

The revelatory power of language is increased if its equivocality is read and seen as one of the properties of that power, as in the case of *muing*. The ambiguity of that word is amplified in Drabble's novel, expressed in such relations as accident and plan, choice and destiny, confinement and liberty, and in regard to the last, more complexly, between what is possible to contemplate when one is confined to a cell, shut away from the world where action is usually precluded—what amounts to the *vita contemplativa* (in medieval thought) as compared to the *vita activa,* the life in the world of actions that is contingent, subject to accident and vicissitudes, where a person's faith in reason and divine plan is always tested. Interestingly, Hannah Arendt explores these issues in her work, especially in *The Human Condition.*

Getting in and out of prison is a major activity in *The Ice Age.* Len Wincobank, Anthony's partner in real estate, spends four years in jail for bad investments and shoddy financial dealings. Alison's elder daughter, Jane, is sentenced to two years in prison in Wallacia, a small, remote, Eastern bloc country, for being involved in an automobile accident in which two people died. Anthony wishes he were where Len Wincobank was so he could give up making choices, but, he thinks, "No guardian angel would put him quietly away in a cell where he could go quietly mad" (225). A little later in the book, Drabble, guardian angel–like, puts him in a cell in a Wallacian prison for six years (after he gets Jane out and onto a plane for England). He does not go mad, but like Boethius, whose *Consolations of Philosophy* he reads over and over in his cell, he writes a book—his about the nature of God. His mind "wonderfully concentrated" from all his deprivations, "he is determined, alone, to justify the ways of God to man." He simply cannot believe that he is in the hands of those "three gray sisters," subject to the "random malice" spun out by fate (294).

Another meaning latent in the word *muing* is "change," "transmuta-
tion." The patterns of change that Anthony goes through bear some
resemblance to those that happened to England in the sixties and seventies. Anthony turned his back on God and philosophy (his father was a
churchman and a schoolmaster in the cathedral school of his ancient
hometown), first for the entertainment world, then for the business
world, in which he was quickly successful, only to return again, after
reversals and a period of confinement, to a reconsideration of philosophy
and especially of God, and thus to a flicker of hope. Similarly, England,
after a period of great development and expansion is experiencing a
slowdown, a freeze, a confinement in an ice age.

> A huge icy fist, with large cold fingers, was squeezing and chilling
> the people of Britain, that great and puissant nation, slowing down
> their blood, locking them into immobility, fixing them into a solid
> stasis, like fish in a frozen river. (*IA* 60)

There is some hope after all. "I think the English are changing" (*IA*
220), declares Giles Peters, Anthony's college friend and another of his
business partners, to Mike Morgan, a comedian whose routines are designed to heap abuse on England and humiliate the English while making
them laugh at it all. As to what the future might be, it seemed to Anthony

> that there would be an answer for the nation, if not for himself, and
> he saw as he sat there, some apparition: of this great and puissant
> nation, a country lying there surrounded by gray seas, the land
> green and gray, well worn, long inhabited, not in chains, not in
> thrall, but a land passing through some strange metamorphosis,
> through the intense creative lethargy of profound self-contempla-
> tion, not idle, not defeated, but waiting still, assembling defenses
> against the noxious oily tides of fatigue and contempt that washed
> insistently against her shores. An aerial view, a helicopter view of
> this precious isle came into his head, and he saw the seas washing
> forever, or more or less forever, around the white and yellow and
> pink and gray sand and pebbles of the beaches, this semi-precious
> stone set in a leaden sea, our heritage, the miles of coast as yet
> unenclosed, not roped and staked and parceled. What next? The
> roping, the selling, the plundering? The view shimmered, frag-
> mented, dissolved like a cloud. The silence lasted. (*IA* 221)

The love of England in Milton's vision exists in the tone of Anthony's, but the loftiness, the grandeur, is gone. The image in the mind's eye requires a helicopter to achieve the distance that reveals England, the island—now a far cry from the empire that the sun once never set on, now the only jewel ("a *semi*-precious stone" [my emphasis]) in its crown—as it lies in a sea that is leaden, laden with the oil beneath its floor. The reduction of vision is pervasive. There are no longer heights for England to reach from which the din cannot be heard. There is no "envious gabble." Even the roar of the quotidian is gone, lost in a lethargy of silence—in engorged moments of waiting for the future.

Drabble dines at Milton's table, but her dinner partner is his ghost, so reduced are the straits that England is in, a condition demonstrated in the lanaguage of her text. The opening of the novel evokes such a reduction, a fall (from grace?), by the juxtaposing of Milton's eagle in the epigraph with a low-flying fowl in the first sentence: "On a Wednesday in the second half of November, a pheasant flying over Anthony Keating's pond, died of a heart attack, as birds sometimes do: it thudded down and fell into the water, where he discovered it some hours later" (*IA* 3). Leaving the vision of the eagle raising its eyes and looking unblinkingly into the midday sun, we arrive at the fictional reality of the pheasant dead in the water. The swift reduction produces vertigo—a falling, like Alice into the tunnel, spinning a serpentine tale out onto the page. But Drabble may be alluding here to another story whose eponymous main character may even be one of the presiding spirits of her book (along with Milton and St. Anthony of monasticism and temptations).

Is it mere coincidence, a trick of the unconscious, or authorial plan that the opening words of *The Ice Age,* "On a Wednesday in the second half of November" (3), are reminiscent of those that open chapter 5 of *Tristram Shandy:* "On the fifth day of November, 1718"? This is the date on which that great patchwork of a fellow was

> brought into this scurvy and disastrous world of ours . . . [only to] have been the continual sport of what the world calls fortune; . . . at every turn and corner where she could get fairly at me, the ungracious Duchess has pelted me with a set of as pitiful misadventures and cross accidents as every small HERO sustained. (Sterne 40)

Not only is Anthony a "small HERO" in his way, buffeted about by dame Fortune, but that busy and "ungracious Duchess" seems to be indulging in a frenzy of activity everywhere, affecting others as well. In his pocket, as he fished the bird out of the pond, is a letter from Kitty Friedmann "which had thudded onto his doormat that morning" (*IA* 3). Kitty and her husband, Max, had been the random targets of an IRA bomb that killed Max and blew off Kitty's foot as they sat dining in a Mayfair restaurant in celebration of their Ruby wedding anniversary: "The whole thing has been a ghastly, arbitrary accident" (*IA* 6). There is nothing connecting the bird's heart attack and Kitty's misfortune except the word *thudded,* used twice to connect Anthony to each of them. The bird "thudded" into his pond (never mind that thudding probably cannot take place in the air), and the letter "thudded" onto his doorstep. Just after the second "thudded," we learn that Anthony's heart has just nearly thudded to a stop, that he is just recovering from a heart attack.

Thudding is part of living, of life, part of the passing of time. Only when time pauses (*IA* 248) does the thudding (heart) stop. Just before Drabble separates them near the end of the novel, in an unusually serene and blissful moment that alludes to an earlier passionate lovemaking scene, a kind of *liebestod,* Anthony and Alison listen to the silence that floods their house. They have the sensation that "time paused: they heard its heart stop, they heard its breath hold, they heard the lapse of thudding and rustling and pumping and beating. They listened to the silence" (*IA* 248).

Whether birds have heart attacks like humans and whether thudding can take place in the air are not important. What is significant is that the connection has been reinforced between Anthony and those to whom these accidents (one natural and the other human-made) occurred. A feeling of uncertainty has been set up, a comic instability established (which ends only at the end of time). Drabble achieves a sense of random connections, or to put it another way, she creates a mesh of disconnections right from the opening of her novel. All her characters are caught in that mesh. The strategy underscores the disconnections, as in the trees and the novelistic mesh, the forest. In the movement of her novel, the reader can see the forest *and* the trees; the reader is given the macrocosmic and the microcosmic views.

Drabble is not always subtle about how the mesh is made. Just after

Anthony buries the bird and reads Kitty's letter, with something of a wink to her readers, she goes so far as to write that Anthony now nurses his heart carefully, "as though it was a child or a bird" (*IA* 6). That she leaves herself open to charges of heavy-handedness or of clumsy and artificial plots does not trouble her. She wants her readers to be aware of the fiction whose truth is, in her words, "beyond the material representation" (Rose, *Critical Essays* 30). She develops characters and personalities to explore her ideas, moves them around to shape those ideas, and does not mind if her readers are wise to her. She encourages it by stepping in every now and then to speak to them directly about the plot, as in the beginning of part 3: "It ought now to be necessary to imagine a future for Anthony Keating. There is no need to worry about the other characters for the present" (*IA* 243). The future perfect is inscribed here as a condition of both the writing and the reading of a novel. These remarks of Drabble's not only are self-referential but compel reflection on the genre as a whole. Later, when Drabble tells us that "life in the immediate *future was* extremely unpleasant for Anthony Keating" (*IA* 280), we can sense the blurriness of the time frame out of which the statement proceeds. The problematic of the postmodern as both experiment and experience is performed by that utterance.

Drabble proceeds to tells us about what has and will happen to Len Wincobank; Kitty Friedmann; Maureen Kirby, Len's former secretary and girlfriend; Derek Ashby, Maureen's new boss and lover; and Ashby's estranged wife, Evelyn. Then, as if she were the voice-over at the end of a soap opera segment, Drabble asks,

> But what of Anthony Keating and Alison Murray? What will they do? Return to London and the vicissitudes of the market? Farm trout or watercress? Donate High Rook House to the Youth Hostel Association, or transform it into a home for the handicapped? Will Alison resume her long abandoned career, will Anthony drink himself to death? (*IA* 243)

No, none of the above will happen. In just a few pages, a few storytelling strokes, Anthony Keating will have become a British spy (to get Jane out of her Wallacian jail) complete with Foreign Office (F. O.) and its operative, Humphrey Clegg, whose suave and low-key official demeanor hides a terrible skeleton in his closet, rather in his suitcase that he keeps in his closet. Anthony suspects him of a homosexuality fostered by public school, but he does not have a clue to the truth that Humphrey Clegg is a solitary transvestite—a secret that when told not only can destroy marriages (as it did Clegg's) but could bring down governments. Clegg was ruined not by Eton but by a maid who would dress him in her frilly blouses and silk underwear, paint his face, and dab him with perfume when he was a little boy. He was imprisoned "by this misfortune in a jail from which there was no release" (*IA* 258). As sobering a thought as this is, the thought of Humphrey Clegg of the F. O. and his secret suitcase is also funny, a comic trill (black comedy, to be sure), a parodic embellishment on flaws and secrets, spies and spying.

The novel in this part takes on the aspect of a scenario, a screenplay of a spy thriller. Both medium and genre are acknowledged by allusion and suggestion—"All the films he [Anthony] had seen and all the thrillers he had read led him to expect a high degree of deviousness for the Foreign Office" (*IA* 253)—and self-reflexively—"anyway Anthony Keating didn't mind if the whole thing was a fake" (*IA* 254). Gathering his courage to face the prison from which he hopes to have Jane released, he tells himself to "emulate Michael Caine and Sean Connery" (281), both high-level celluloid spies. Putting Anthony up for the night, Clegg gives him a John le Carré (of *The Spy Who Came in from the Cold* fame) novel to read, whose obscure plot our "HERO" could not follow.

> He finished the John *le Carré* in a couple of hours, still not quite sure what had happened in the course of the *plot*. He then embarked on the Theban plays of *Sophocles* which he had also packed in his bag. (*IA* 282; my emphasis)

The three words *plot, Sophocles,* and *le Carré* each say plot in one way or another. Sophocles' play *Oedipus,* the primal whodunit, is the basis for Aristotle's definition of plot. And *le Carré,* a French pen name for David John Cornwell, means a "four-sided figure" according to the French dictionary, a square of land that in English is called a plot, and it names a person who writes intrigues—*l'intrigue* is a French equivalent for plot. *The Ice Age* is a parody of the highly plotted novel.

The plot is revealed to be a scam, a rook only if the reader wants to connive with the author. Such connivance is risky, because once an author's words are not taken at face value, the reader cannot be sure what his or her attitude is supposed to be, nor is there any certainty about what the author's attitude is. This, according to Northrop Frye, is the condition of irony (223). Listening to the stories that Tim, an actor friend of Alison's tells, Anthony thinks about the relation of stories and lies and realizes that he is bored with them because they are all lies.

> He had never gone much for the theory that good storytellers never have any respect for the truth. On the contrary, he tended to think that only the truth could possibly be interesting. However dull the truth, it was more interesting than a fantasy. (*IA* 146)

Troubled and disturbed by Tim, "a strange desire to protect him from his own lies came over . . . [Anthony]: he had entered into connivance" (*IA* 146), and he began to nod in agreement with him and to facilitate his lies (stories). In this self-reflexive moment in the novel, the reader can take Drabble at her word that "the truth is more interesting than fantasy" and that Anthony's connivance is pejorative, but only when he or she can forget that Drabble does not authorize such forgetting. For her, the plot is a device for the contemplation of, a mulling over of, the implications of the reading and the writing that is going on and of the issues of plot itself—the relation of plan and accident.

"There is no such thing as accident. We are all marked down. We choose what our own ill thoughts choose for us," thinks Alison in the plane taking her back to England after she saw her daughter Jane in the foreign prison (*IA* 155). The thought is prompted by her recollection of an accident in which Jane at age seven nearly lost an eye in what may have been a bid "for attention. . . . Or for equality?" (*IA* 155). That was the year Jane suffered the inevitable displacement that accompanies the birth of a sibling, which in her case was drastically complicated because Molly, her new sister, was severely damaged by cerebral palsy. "Had she lost an eye, as she so nearly managed to do so, that would have evened the score between Molly and Jane. An eye for an eye. A sacrificial gesture, rather than a gesture of spite," reflects Allison, as she mulls over the possibilities (*IA* 155). "No," she concludes, "one must continue to behave as though one believed in the accidental. That shows our greatest faith. Molly's fate is an accident, not a retribution. So I must see it" (*IA* 155). Molly's fate is inexorably Alison's too. About her relation to Molly, Alison knew that "she loved her hopelessly, tenderly. At times it seemed worthwhile. At other times not so. Either way there was no choice. It was so" (*IA* 107).

Alison thinks a lot about accident, destiny, and choice. Now in her middle years, her hair graying, but still a beautiful woman, she faces a life that by any measure would appear unduly burdened and compromised. Her marriage failed. One of her children, Molly, is so defective that she can only do a few simple tasks for herself, speak only minimally (assessing her IQ is impossible), and eat and move only with extreme difficulty. She is beginning to dislike her other child, Jane, now grown, who is in jeopardy in a Balkan jail. She abandoned her career just as it began to flourish, partly because of Molly, partly to stop competing with her ex-husband, also an actor (it did not help). Her lover (Anthony) has just had a heart attack and faces bankruptcy. And her sister, Rosemary, long jealous of her beauty, is deformed by a mastectomy. Alison's catalog of woes leads the reader to question her conclusion, to meditate especially on the possibility that it may be too easy to ascribe it all to accident. Alison has made some choices in these matters, choices that are not always made by conscious means alone.

But what is choice? "Choice stands in the place of necessity, of destiny. Thus man overcomes death, which in thought he [man] has acknowledged," writes Freud in his paper on "The Theme of the Three Caskets," in which he considers how contradictions are often represented by a single element in modes of expression used by the unconscious, such as dreams. After analyzing various myths, tales, and other works concerned with wishes and choices, giving special attention to "The Judgment of Paris," the casket scene from *The Merchant of Venice,* and Lear's choice of daughters, Freud notices the

> acme of contradiction. . . . Every time there occurs a free choice between the women [in the works referred to above], and if the choice is thereupon to fall on death—that which no man chooses, to which by destiny alone man falls a victim. (72)

That is to say, humans chose their destiny. An ancient ambivalence manifested, for example, in deities of dual natures of fertility and destruction, or of love and death, accounts for such contradictions and anticipates the mental activity Freud called the reaction-formation, the replacement of something with its opposite. In this case, the reaction-formation occurs to satisfy rebellious wishes against subjection to the immutable law of death guarded by the Fates, *Moirai,* who relentlessly spin and cut the thread of life.

The beautiful and talented Alison Murray has seen Anthony

through a heart attack and has moved away from London with him to the north, where it is quieter and prettier, but not necessarily better. The bottom has dropped out of Anthony's business ventures, and the country's economy and the immediate future seem perilous. When the book opens, Alison has left High Rook House for Wallacia to see Jane through her ordeal—an unsuccessful and trying attempt. The rift between the nineteen-year-old Jane and her mother is so wide and so filled with poor Molly that it keeps each of them from taking any emotional solace from the other. So Alison leaves Jane in her prison cell; she can do nothing for her anymore. Now there is just Molly. Returning to High Rook House, Alison sees Anthony caring for Molly devotedly, lovingly, with obvious pleasure, and she becomes jealous of him. Her pain is so acute, and with all she has been through, she suffers a collapse. For Alison, there can be no separating from Molly.

At the end of the novel, after she has saved his financial skin and has turned him into a British spy, Drabble puts Anthony into a prison cell, where he suffers and thinks and writes. Toward the end of his second year, he sees a rare bird, a tree creeper (he knows what kind it is from a book of European birds that he asked for and got), and "he experiences hope" (*IA* 295)—"'Hope' is the thing with feathers" (Dickinson 116); "He experiences joy. The bird will fly off, fluttering away its tiny life. There we leave Anthony" (*IA* 295). In an envoi, the ending after the end of the book, Drabble writes:

> Alison there is no leaving. Alison can neither live nor die. Alison has Molly. Her life is beyond imagining. It will not be imagined. Britain will recover, but not Alison Murray. (*IA* 295)

—whose name announces *Moira.*

"*Alison there is no leaving. Alison can neither live nor die.*" She is the figure of *Moira*, the living inexorably toward death. In Heidegger's words, "*Moira* is the destining of the disclosure of duality" (100). The use of the gerundive noun, hallmark of Heideggerian style, indicates the process, the what is going on—in his words again, the "presencing of what is present" (98)—which can only be unveiled, unconcealed, as an effect of seeing. Meaning is revealed after—*nachträglich*—looking back. *Moira*, unpresentable, is difference manifested in Molly.

"*Alison has Molly.*" An accident of fate, Anthony

felt quite strongly that she [Molly] has the misfortune to be intelligent enough to experience acutely her own disabilities. . . . Her fits of rage were fits of intense frustration at her own inability to do the things she felt she ought to do. (*IA* 143)

In her psychosocial development, Molly is marooned in the mirror stage, Lacan's well-known formulation of the instance of the ego, forever seeing her alienated image without being able to grab onto that "line of fiction,"[9] with which to close the gap between her and herself (however asymptotic the result must always be). She remains in front of the mirror with Alison, her *trotte-bébé,* to use Lacan's phrase, her physical support, stuck in a "real" that is unrepresentable, that does not exist except as a blur, an effect of a chiasmic and multidimensional relation that consists, theoretically speaking, of the Lacanian registers of the imaginary and the symbolic intersecting the actual and the fictional. That blur could be considered a *moiré* effect of *Moira,* a Derridian homophonic pun set up to suggest the shaking up of destiny—the double genitive here, both the shaking and the being shaken. Without that (life)line of fiction, that access to the order of language, Molly is lost to the blur of the real.

"*Alison has Molly. Her life is beyond imagining.*" Whose life? Alison's most likely, but then so is Molly's. The ambiguity is deliberate. The two lives have become so imbricated that they are one.

"*It will not be imagined.*" It is not the stuff of fiction. Yet, undeterred, as if responding to a conundrum, an impossible demand, as in Beckett's "Imagination Dead Imagine," Drabble imagines Molly through the subtlety of her onomastic skills, by naming Alison's "poor lump" of a child (*IA* 151), who must be mollycoddled all her life, Molly. Mary Lydon, writing of another, more famous fictional Molly, reminds us that Molly is a namesake of "that fabulous herb moly which preserved Odysseus from being turned into one of Circe's swine." As Lydon suggests that Joyce's Molly "might be taken as a specific, a medicine to protect women from imprisonment in the real of their own sexuality, in the image of the mother's body, cut off from the heterotopia of the symbolic" ("Foucault and Feminism" 247), so I suggest that Drabble's Molly (so utterly different from Joyce's and yet enough like her to also rage a "yes" to life) is Alison's specific, in the special case of *pharmakon,* also equivocal as remedy and poison, but one that keeps her imprisoned in the real of Molly's insufficiency.

So *"Britain will recover, but not Alison Murray."* Even so, Alison chooses Molly again and again, over her career, over her other daughter, and perhaps even over her lover. According to Alison, the facts are: "There is no comfort, no sustenance. But who can be surprised that one so subject to the blows of circumstance should attempt to see them in a possibility of self-will, freedom, choice?" (247). Freud understands these consolations: "No greater triumph of wish fulfillment is conceivable. Just where in reality he [humankind] obeys compulsion, he exercises choice; and that which he chooses is not a thing of horror, but the fairest and most desirable thing in life" (73). Both Alison and Anthony appear to have made their choices.

The envoi is a sending forth, an apocalypse: "The end is the beginning" (Derrida, "Of an Apocalyptic Tone" 84). The envoi is also a return. Our epigraphic eagle looking unblinkingly into the sun is the envisioning of a vision so clear and radiant that all is revealed. Anthony, walking toward the prison in Wallacia, "stopped in the roadway, like Paul on the way to Damascus," to think about God: "I do not know how man can do without God." The realization did not overwhelm him, because, Drabble writes, "alas, faith had not accompanied the concept" (*IA* 265). This moment was not for revelations anyway, we are told, because "it was hot: the late spring sun beat down fiercely on his bare head. Mad dogs and Englishmen, reflected Anthony Keating" (*IA* 265). The noonday sun is impossible to look at, especially with eyes "undazl'd and unscal[ed]"; at least one eye must be closed. A certain connivance with the vision must take place. The etymology of *connive* is "to wink at." Hence, one must wink at the vision to find it. There is irony in connivance, and the wink is comic. The postmodern condition is here— the condition in which *The Ice Age* was written.

With Drabble at Milton's gala,[10] we are absorbed with her vision that defines itself not so much in "methinks I see" but in "methinks," a thinking heard in the mind, a prognostication of sects and schisms, but also a tone—a strange and uncertain mesh—of a possibility and, in a latent meaning of *apocalypse,* a contemplation.

Chapter 3

Marguerite Duras

If thou didst hold me in thy heart,
absent thee from felicity awhile,
And in this harsh world draw thy breath in pain,
to tell my story.

—*Hamlet* 5.2

When Marguerite Duras was asked if she believed that an image was worth a thousand words, she replied: "No. A word contains a thousand images." The word, according to Duras, has "the power of proliferation" ("la puissance de prolifération"), a power that the image contains also but to "an infinitely lesser degree" ("infiniment moins grande" [*DM* 45]). The images that are compacted into words are not just pictures that may move on a screen or make telling compositions on the stage. They are the material that give form to the forgotten, to the unconscious—to history. Words for Duras are written spaces (she has called them *les trous*, "holes" [*Le ravissement de Lol V. Stein* 48]) that contain the time of love and death. They are those absences and mental images through which we see ourselves. They contain her stories, which become history.

In Marguerite Duras's *Hiroshima mon amour*, the relation of history and story becomes a structure of relations that traverses the distance between the history of unspeakable death that is Hiroshima and the story of love that happened there one day in the summer of 1957. Hiroshima is history; *Hiroshima mon amour* is *her* story. The knot between history and her story in Duras's screenplay does not simply consist in the placing of a story about the chance meeting of two people who fall in love against the background of a city recovering from the ravages of World War II. It is the effort to write about the impossibility of writing about

Hiroshima, an impossible place whose name silently shrieks holocaust, a place of impossibility that nevertheless persists as a locus through which the axes of history and story, space and time, and love and death intersect as do the lives of the lovers. Through the words of the text offering the embrace, the play of emotions between the woman and man, the rest is revealed.

Duras is definite about this.

> Toujours leur histoire personelle, aussi courte soi-telle, l'emportera sur HIROSHIMA.
> Si cette condition n'était pas tenue, ce film, encore une fois, ne serait qu'un film de commande de plus, sans aucun intérêt sauf celui d'un documentaire romance. Si cette condition est tenue, on aboutira à une espèce de *faux documentaire* qui sera bien plus probant de la leçon de HIROSHIMA qu'un documentaire de commande. (*Hma* 12; my emphasis)

> (Their personal story, however brief it may be, always dominates Hiroshima.
> If this premise were not adhered to, this would be just one more made-to-order picture of no more interest than any fictionalized documentary. If it is adhered to, we'll end up with a sort of *false documentary* that will probe the lesson of Hiroshima more deeply than any made-to-order documentary.) (*HMA* 10; my emphasis)

Duras makes an acute distinction between fictionalized documentary, contrived to be made to the order of the genre documentary that shows and records reality so truth can be ascertained, and false documentary, which does not produce documentation that is evidence or proof but remains a documentary that, according to its etymological strains, is a means of teaching and learning "that will probe the lesson of Hiroshima."

To replace a screenplay he had found unacceptable, the film's director, Alain Resnais, asked Duras to write one about Hiroshima in three weeks. Reeling from the enormity of the assignment, she decided that rather than risking the impudence and the vulgarity of bearing witness to such an atrocity—"un événement de cette envergure, de cette dimension, de ce qui est le plus grand événement du XXe siècle, avec les camps de concentration" (an event of such scope and dimension that it is, along with the concentration camps, the greatest event of the twentieth century [*DM* 26–27])—she would say nothing at all about Hiroshima. After all, what could she say? What could be said? Instead, she attempted to discover the experience of Hiroshima by indirection, by circumvention; she experimented. She found the event by the invention of a story of the most ordinary kind—a love story. But as Duras writes:

> Cette étreinte, si banale, si quotidienne, a lieu dans la ville du monde où elle est le plus difficile à imaginer: HIROSHIMA. Rien n'est "donne" à HIROSHIMA. Un halo particulier y auréole chaque geste, chaque parole, d'un sens supplémentaire à leur sens litteral. (*Hma* 11)

> (Their embrace—so banal, commonplace—takes place in the one city in the world where it is hardest to imagine it: Hiroshima. Nothing is "given" in Hiroshima. Every gesture, every word takes on an aura of meaning that transcends its literal meaning. [*HMA* 9])

When set in Hiroshima, even the most ordinary story is, as if in an alembic, transmuted into something more—into history.

To borrow Freud's formulation in *Beyond the Pleasure Principle* that life is a circuitous route to death, so is the story a circuitous route to history. The suggestion of the circle is not gratuitous here. The scenario will unfold, and the beginning will have been difficult to pinpoint; it will have ended in impossibility, the way it began. It will have been another detour, another loop in time, a circulation of story and history. The future anterior is the tense of invention, a finding afterward of what came before. It announces a postmodern criticism of representation: the problem of writing the remains, those glimpses of what is already a forgotten and unyielding past. Duras's stories are the remnants that remain to be written out of the silence of an unspeakable night. Hannah Arendt might have thought of them as remembrances that reconcile the past (bring understanding), as the mastering of (past) moments. But notions of mastery, although her stories may bear evidence of them, are not readily applicable to Duras's style, whose most insistent impulse is to disappear into the page.

The story of *Hiroshima mon amour* is as brief as the encounter. It is comprised of only two characters, the man and the woman, whose names we never learn. We know them only as he and she. They have met, we are not told how, on the last day of the shooting of an international film on peace, set in Hiroshima, in which the woman, a French actress, plays a nurse. He is a Japanese architect interested in politics. He speaks fluent French, which he says he learned so he could read about the French revolution. They are both in their early thirties, handsome, and cosmopolitan. Their first embrace is passionate but seemingly casual, which, in spite of themselves, swells into love, uselessly and hopelessly because she is leaving for the other side of the world, for Paris, the next day, and because they are each happily married with families.

"Theirs was a one-night affair" (*HMA* 9)—but with a difference of course. The difference is history. Before the night is over, the French woman tells her lover of another impossible love, a story long buried and forgotten that she has never told anyone else, of Nevers in France, where she was young and in love for the first time, and where she was mad for a while. As they sit over a drink in an all-night cafe, she tells him randomly, in bits and pieces, about Nevers, where she fell in love with a German soldier during the occupation; about how one day when the war was nearly over, she hurried to meet him on the quay of the Loire, from where they would leave for Bavaria to marry. When she got to the quay, she found him shot—not quite dead yet. She stayed with him for a day and night, not knowing when he died, until they came and took him away in a truck. Then they shaved her head in the town square, and she went mad with grief and hate. Her mother and father put her in the cellar of their house, until one day she was less mad and her hair had grown back. Then her mother told her she would have to leave for Paris by night on her bicycle. Two days later, she arrived to find news about Hiroshima in all the newspapers on the streets of Paris.

As he and she sit huddled together in the cafe, heads and hands touching, and he helps her unravel the thread of memory, the time they have left together in Hiroshima seems to disappear. He says, "Il ne nous reste plus maintenant qu'à tuer le temps qui nous sépare de ton départ" (*Hma* 83). ("All we can do now is kill time before your departure" [*HMA* 52].) They carry out the figure of speech literally, because he becomes the dead lover as she talks to him.

> LUI: Quand tu es dans la cave, je suis mort?
> ELLE: Tu es mort . . . et . . .
>   . . . Je t'appelle doucement. . . .
> LUI: Mais je suis mort.
> ELLE: Je t'appelle quand même. Même mort.

Puis un jour, tout à coup, je crie, je crie
très fort comme une sourde. . . .

LUI: Tu cri quoi?

ELLE: Ton nom allemand. Seulement ton nom. Je n'ai plus qu'une
seule mémoire, celle de ton nom. . . .

Je n'en peux plus d'avoir envie de toi.

LUI: Tu as peur?

ELLE: J'ai peur. . . .

LUI: De quoi?

ELLE: De ne plus te revoir, jamais, jamais. . . .

Je pense à toi. Mais je ne le dis plus.

LUI: Folle.

ELLE: Je suis folle d'amour de toi. . . .

(Hma 87–95)

(HE: When you are in the cellar, am I dead?

SHE: You are dead . . . and . . .

. . . I call you softly. . . .

HE: But I'm dead.

SHE: Nevertheless I call you. Even though you're dead. Then one
day I scream, I scream as loud as I can, like a deaf person
would. . . .

HE: What do you scream?

SHE: Your German name. Only your name. I only have one memory left, your name. . . .

I want you so badly I can't bear it anymore.

HE: Are you afraid?

SHE: I am afraid. . . .

HE: Of what?

SHE: Of not ever seeing you again. Ever, ever.

. . . I think of you, but I don't talk about it anymore.

HE: Mad.

SHE: Madly in love with you. . . .

[HMA 54–61])

Time no longer exists here. It is the Proustian solution that, according to Samuel Beckett in *Proust,* "consists in the negation of Time and
Death, the negation of Death because the negation of Time. Death is
dead because Time is dead." Beckett considers *le temps retrouvé* an inappropriate description of the Proustian solution. He insists that "time is

not recovered, it is obliterated" (56). In Duras's text, the time between the tale and the telling falls away, as does the space. Nevers is resurrected in Hiroshima, and Hiroshima is there in her recollection of Nevers. When the telling stops, time is recovered, but it is not enough.

> LUI: Peut-être que c'est possible, que tu restes.
> ELLE: Tu le sais bien. Plus impossible encore que de se quitter.
> LUI: Huit jours.
> ELLE: Non.
> LUI: Trois jours.
> ELLE: Le temps de quoi? D'en vivre? D'en mourir?
> LUI: Le temps de le savoir.
> ELLE: Ça n'existe pas. Ni le temps d'en vivre. Ni le temps d'en
>   mourir. Alors, je m'en fous.
> LUI: J'aurais préféré que tu sois morte à Nevers.
> ELLE: Moi aussi. Mais je ne suis pas morte à Nevers.
>   (*Hma* 116–17)

> (HE: Maybe it's possible for you to stay.
> SHE: You know it's not. Still more impossible than to leave.
> HE: A week.
> SHE: No.
> HE: Three days.
> SHE: Time enough for what? To live from it? To die from it?
> HE: Time enough to know which.
> SHE: That doesn't exist. Neither time enough to live from it. Nor
>   time enough to die from it. So I don't give a damn.
> HE: I would have preferred that you had died in Nevers.
> SHE: So would I. But I didn't die in Nevers.
>   [*HMA* 77–78])

That is her failure, that she did not die of love on the banks of the Loire in 1944. Duras explains that the story the woman tells of this lost opportunity to die literally transports her outside herself and carries her toward this new man. She delivers to this Japanese in Hiroshima what is dearest to her in all the world: her survival of the death of her love in Nevers (*HMA* 112).

That failure, that lost opportunity, expressed as repetition, makes her love in Hiroshima both strange and familiar—the return of the repressed. The Japanese, finally understanding what her love consists in, says to her:

> Dans quelques années, quand je t'aurai oubliée, et que d'autres histoires comme celle-là, par la force encore de l'habitude, arriveront encore, je me souviendrai de toi comme de l'oublier de l'amour même. Je penserai à cette histoire comme à l'horreur de l'oubli. Je le sais déjà. (*Hma* 105)

> (In a few years, when I'll have forgotten you, and when other such adventures, from sheer habit, will happen to me, I'll remember you as the [forgetting of love itself. I will think of this story as the horror of forgetfulness.] I already know it. [*HMA* 68; translation amended])

The memory of forgetting and the forgotten so imbricated in love, in the endless substitutions for lost loves—for one lost before love—that staves off death in a *scheherezaderie,* is the very stuff of history.

In the last moments of the text, the forgetting is already taking place. In an outburst, the Frenchwoman cries: "Je t'oublierai! Je t'oublie déjà! Regarde, comme je t'oublie! Regarde-moi!" (*Hma* 124). (I'll forget you! I'm forgetting you already! Look how I'm forgetting you! Look at me! [*HMA* 83].) The directions read:

> . . . [elle] l'appelle tout à coup très doucement. Elle l'appelle "au loin," dans l'émerveillement. Elle a réussi à le noyer dans l'oubli universel. Elle en est émerveillée.
> ELLE: Hi-ro-shi-ma.
>   Hi-ro-shi-ma. C'est ton nom.
> LUI: C'est mon nom. Oui. Ton nom à toi est Nevers. Ne-vers-en-Fran-ce.
>
> (Hma 124)

> (. . . suddenly [she calls him softly.] She calls him from afar, lost in wonder. She has succeeded in [submerging] him in universal [forgetfulness. She is filled with the wonder of it.]
> SHE: Hi-ro-shi-ma.
>   Hi-ro-shi-ma. That's your name.

HE: That's my name. Yes. Your name is Nevers.

Ne-vers-in France.

[*HMA* 83; translation amended])

Hiroshima and Nevers come together in the loss of time and space, in a never-never land of lost love—of loss itself.

Much of Duras's work consists in the attempt to inscribe that loss in an elliptical writing that is marked by loss, by omission, by incompleteness. What is lost is only glimpsed at times, never found. Hers can be seen as a ravaged writing about ravishment, a state that she so definitively captures in *Le ravissement de Lol V. Stein*. Duras's writing is so reticent and spare that it is as if she were afraid of being skewered by the very words she writes. *Le ravissement de Lol V. Stein* is a calculus of uncertainty. One of the few things that the reader can depend on in that vertiginous narrative is the appearance over and over again of the name: "Lol V. Stein—c'était ainsi qu'elle se désignait" (*RLVS* 23). (Lol V. Stein—this was the way she referred to herself.[1]) The name itself becomes, for the reader, a material support, a handle (pun intended) that can be grasped, held on to for an instant or two. As Sanford S. Ames puts it, "Lol V. Stein is a pretense (*feinte*) or forgetting fissure (*feinte oublieuse*), she de-signs, her signature is there before and after love, the name without the person, the fiction, the letters of desire" ("Cinderella's Slipper" 247).

As if in an effort to (re)discover itself, the name insists in the story, which is haunted by Lol V. Stein's forgotten memory of a ball during which her fiancé, Michael Richardson, is lost to her forever, as she, astonished, watches an excluding and unrelenting love envelop him and a stranger, Anne-Marie Stretter. At the moment that she sees her exclusion from their intense love, the ravishing (in its double meaning of "violation," i.e., seizing and carrying away, and "rapture") of Lola Valerie Stein has taken place. She is split, erased, leaving only a trace. It is a double erasure, because the memory of that moment is also erased, and her life is a series of repetitions that are the substitutions for the obliterating scene. What is left is Lol V. Stein, caught between violence and ecstasy: "Elle souhaite une interruption dans la sempiternelle répétition de la vie" (*RLVS* 145). (She yearns for an interruption in the neverending repetition of her life.) But it is a vain yearning: she remains outside, unseen, watching in the rye fields of love. There is only an insistent lack and the return of the repressed. This haunting, haunted, sempiternally unfulfilled desire permeates Duras's lettered texts.

Reading the letters—and the names—in these texts is indispensable, and they have been given provocative readings by Ames, among others, and by Lacan (who we already know takes letters literally). Lacan writes of *Le ravissement* in his "Hommage" to Duras: "Lol V. Stein: ailes [pronounced like the letter *L* or the word *elle*] de papier, V, ciseau, Stein, la pierre, au jeu de la mourre tu te perds" (131). (Lol V. Stein: wings of paper, V, scissors, Stein, stone, in the game of love [and chance] you lose yourself.)[2] This signal reading of the letters and the name is inscribed in the writing, in Duras's present tense that whirls around between past and future: "Le lendemain est là. . . . Maintenant, le présent, le seul présent, qui tournoie, tournoie dans la poussière et qui se pose enfin dans le cri, le doux cri aux ailes brisées dont la fêlure n'est perceptible qu'à Lol V. Stein" (*RLVS* 74). (Tomorrow is here. . . . Now, the present, the only present turns round and round, whirling in the dust, and settles finally in the cry, the soft cry of broken wings whose crack is perceptible only to Lol V. Stein.) Ames's elaboration of Lacan's reading and Duras's text is germane: "The wings are cut by the V emblem of writing as castration of the anteriority of the feminine and is followed by the sibilant petrification of Stein" ("Cinderella's Slipper" 248). *V* is understood here as a feminine configuration—covering for the mons veneris, the delta, letter and source of life—and also as one of the consonants of the English word *loves* as in L.V.S.—in Duras's *La femme du Ganges,* Lol V. Stein disappears further into L.V.S.

In *le cri, le doux cri,* "we find the written, *l'écrit,* the gagged scream of writing, the vertigo of being turned into residue, into letters" ("Cinderella's Slipper" 248). The bilingual and ironic name of Lol's lover, and the narrator of the story, is another example of Duras's "materful" onomastics. His name is Jacques Hold, but he does not have hold of very much, not of Lol, not even of the telling of the story, about which he suffers keenly at every turn. He sees, supposes, tells what he has been told (but not too much), imagines, and invents: "J'accepte l'autre [fin], celle qui est à inventer, que je ne connais pas, que personne encore n'a inventée: la fin sans fin, le commencement sans fin de Lol V. Stein" (*RLVS* 184). (I accept the other [end], still to be invented, the end I don't know, that no one has invented yet: the endless end, the endless beginning of Lol V. Stein.)

In *Beyond the Pleasure Principle,* Freud wrote that repetition, especially the repetition of unpleasurable experience, usually yields pleasure because of the passivity of the experience. Men and women are flailed by experience; experiences happen *to* them: incidents, events, catastrophes, holocausts. When these are repeated (among children it is called play, among adults, art), the passivity of the experience becomes the activity of the repetition, and pleasure is produced. Even women, who have been identified as passive—an identification that Freud warned was facile and unproductive (see p. 40)—find that such activity gives them pleasure (12–17).

La ravissement mandates the anguish of writing: how to tell the story (Drabble's problem, too, as we have seen). Jacques Hold's narrative voice is, in Lacan's words, "its anguish" ("son angoisse"). Any possible ambiguity here is not lost on Lacan, who asks, "Is it his [anguish] or that of the narrative's?" ("Hommage" 132). There can be no separation between the two, and the anguish is also Duras's. She has Jacques Hold write that he believes that Lol is silent because she is looking for a "word-hole (un mot-trou [a "true" word?]), . . . a hole in which all the other words would have been buried" ([un] trou où tous les autres mots auraient été enterrés [*RLVS* 48]) that is not there, but that he believes might be there anyway. Jacques continues:

> Ce mot, qui n'existe pas, pourtant est là: il vous attend au tournant du langage, il vous défie, il n'a jamais servi, de le soulever, de le faire surgir hors de son royaume percé de toutes parts à travers lequel s'écoulent la mer, le sable, l'éternité du bal dans le cinéma de Lol V. Stein. (*RLVS* 48–49)

> (This word that does not exist is nonetheless there: it waits around the bend of language, it defies you—being never used—to raise it, to make it surge out of its kingdom of which every part is pierced and through which flows the sea, the sand, and the eternity of the ball in the cinema of Lol V. Stein.)

That "kingdom" (*royaume*) is the unconscious to which writing, like the dream, may be a royal road. The desire to write is ambushed at every turn by the impulse not to. Jacques Hold says: "Je voudrais faire, dire, dire un long mugissement fait de tous mots fondus et revenus au même magma, intelligible à Lol V. Stein. Je me tais. Je dis: . . . " (*RLVS* 130). (I should like to make a long roar of all words melted down to the same magma, intelligible to Lol V. Stein. I say nothing. I say: . . .) Saying nothing is as impossible as saying something. The long roar, both empty and full at the same time, both anonymous and particular, is the cry that is delayed and deferred in writing (echoes of the cry, the howl, that Bernard longs for in Woolf's *The Waves*). *L'éCRIt* (writing) is all that is left of the cry (*le cri*). Visually (in French) and literally, the cry is there (*là*), but it is smudged out, like Lola, in the writing. It is the remembering of the forgotten.

The telling of the story is inscribed in the scenario of *Hiroshima mon amour*, just as it is in *Le ravissement* and in most of Duras's other texts. In *Hiroshima*, the Frenchwoman tells the stories; the Japanese man tells none. *Hiroshima mon amour* is her story, and Duras's. In an interior monologue, the woman speaks to her dead lover: "Je t'ai trompé ce soir avec cet inconnu. J'ai raconté notre histoire. Elle était, vois-tu, racontable" (*Hma* 110). (I was unfaithful to you tonight with this stranger. I told him our story. It was, you see, a story that could be told [*HMA* 73]). Every love is a love story. The words of love (*les mots d'amour*) are its names; the places of that love are its geography: "You are Hi-ro-shi-ma"; "You are Ne-vers-in-France." Duras's words of love and fiction are Lahore, Venice, Calcutta, Chandernagore, Mekong, Paris, Savannakhet, Ganges, Siam, and always beaches, islands, and oceans. In Duras's play, *Savannah Bay*, (in which Edith Piaf's famous rendering of "Les mots d'amour" has a prominent role), Madeleine wonders what love without a story would be.

In *Hiroshima mon amour*, the story was meant to be told. When the Frenchwoman was coming back from where her madness had taken her in that cellar in Nevers, she said:

> Je commence à voir.
> Je me souviens avoir déjà vu—avant—avant—pendant que nous nous aimions, pendant notre bonheur.
> Je me souviens.
> *Je vois l'encre.*
> Je vois le jour.
> Je vois ma vie. Ta mort.
> Ma vie qui continue. Ta mort qui continue. . . .
> (*Hma* 98; my emphasis)

> (I'm beginning to see.
> I remember having already seen before—before—when we were in love, when we were happy.

I remember.
I see the ink.
I see the daylight.
I see my life. Your death.
My life that goes on. Your death that goes on. . . . (*HMA* 63; my emphasis)

What ink did she see? The ink that would become the smudge, the grapheme, the story: "histoire de quatre sous" (*Hma* 118) (a three-penny story [*HMA* 79]), as she calls it. When she sees, when she remembers, she is already written. She sees the ink of her text—the ink of story and history by which she will have (re)discovered her experience.

Eudora Welty, in her *One Writer's Beginnings,* offers a striking word to describe the relation between experience and literary invention. That word is *confluence.* To demonstrate what this word discloses, she quotes from a scene in her novel *The Optimist's Daughter,* in which hero and heroine, traveling by train, look down in the early morning, from an aqueduct, and see the confluence of the Ohio and Mississippi Rivers. "All they saw," writes Welty, "was at the point of coming together . . . the rivers moving into one. . . . All they could see was sky, water, birds, light, and confluence" (103). Welty concludes *One Writer's Beginnings:*

> Of course the greatest confluence of all is that which makes up the human memory—the individual human memory. My own is the treasure most dearly regarded by me, in my life and in my work as a writer. Here time, also, is subject to confluence. But during its moment, all that is remembered joins, and lives—the old and the young, the past and the present, the living and the dead. (104)

Welty's word is particularly resonant because confluence not only means the flowing together of the waters but hints at the flowing of language. In the writing of the forgotten and the remembered, in the confluence of time, in the invention, something is found out.

The desire to know, that Oedipal desire, permeates Duras's *Le vice-consul,* a novel eerily reminiscent of Greek tragedy. Little happens besides the movement of the characters. The mad beggar woman's impossible trek from Savannakhet to Calcutta winds around the comings and goings, the assemblings and reassemblings, of the functionaries, who are the white colonials in the mid-1930s. The people talk somewhat in the manner of a Greek chorus, repeating scraps of information known about the French vice-consul and Anne-Marie Stretter, the French ambassador's wife. For the most part, they ask questions about them and give answers that are usually wrong, but sometimes not. It is hard to know.

The question asked most often is why did the vice-consul go mad and shoot at the lepers in the Shalimar Gardens. No conclusive reasons are given, and the vice-consul adamantly refuses to provide any in his deposition: "Simplement, je me borne ici à constater l'impossibilité où je suis de rendre compte de façon comprehensible de ce qui s'est passé à Lahore" (*VC* 39). (Simply put, I can only state here the impossibility of giving any comprehensible account of what happened in Lahore.) He takes full responsibility for what he has done and is ready to accept whatever consequences are meted out. Yet he cannot quite see himself and the doer of those deeds in Lahore as identical. He speaks of himself in the third person, as if to separate himself—the man at the embassy reception dancing with Anne-Marie Stretter, with whom he is now hopelessly in love—from the man who went berserk in the Shalimar Gardens: "Je voudrais essayer de vous dire, après, on sait que c'est soi qui était à Lahore dans l'impossibilité d'y être. C'est moi qui... celui qui vous parle en ce moment... c'est lui" (*VC* 126). (I would like to try to tell you that afterwards, although one knows that it was oneself who was in Lahore, being there seems an impossibility. It is I who... the one who speaks to you at this moment... it is he.)

Desperate and powerful in his desire for Anne Marie Stretter to understand about Lahore all at once—without details, without rationalizations—the vice-consul commands her attention.

> Lahore, c'était encore une forme de l'espoir. Vous comprenez n'est-ce pas?... Essayez... je vous en supplie, d'apercevoir Lahore.... Il est huit heures du matin, les jardins de Shalimar sont déserts. Je ne sais pas que vous existez vous aussi.... je voudrais que vous disiez que vous apercevez le côté inévitable de Lahore. Répondez-moi. (*VC* 126–27)

> (Lahore was still a kind of hope. You do understand, don't you?... Try... I implore you to see [perceive] Lahore.... It is eight o'clock in the morning. The Shalimar Gardens are deserted. I don't know that you, too, exist.... I would like you to say that you see [perceive] the inevitability of Lahore. Answer me.)

He has already intuited her knowledge of Lahore, but he must have her
admit it to him. As if submitting to the force of his desire, she says: "Je
l'aperçois le côté inévitable de Lahore. . . . Je l'apercevais déjà hier mais
je ne le savais pas" (*VC* 128). (I see the inevitability of Lahore. I saw it
yesterday, but I didn't know it.)

Lahore is what they know about each other. Their love is bound
up with Lahore, and like Lahore, it is inevitable and impossible. It cannot
be recounted. It is *hors texte*—literally unpaginated material. It is there
but not there, uncounted, like the vice-consul and India, who were
everywhere alone and ignored: "On ignore le vice-consul et il l'admet.
Debout, il se tait. De même sur l'Inde. Sur l'Inde comme sur lui, pas
un mot n'est dit" (*VC* 107). (The vice-consul is ignored, and he is re-
signed to it. He stands there, silent. It is the same with India. India, like
him, is ignored.)

Perhaps after Lahore the vice-consul is *hors la loi,* an outlaw; perhaps
not. He is recalled to Calcutta while awaiting reassignment, and neither
he nor Lahore are subject to legal procedures. They are outside the reach
of the court. Charles Rossett realizes the effort that the French ambassador is making to find some excuse for the vice-consul's behavior and
asks if this is not a straightforward case that calls for exemplary punish-
ment. The ambassador suggests that the matter is not as serious as was
first thought and eliminates the possibility of a case being brought to
trial: "Ici, il n'y a pas de partie adverse, n'est-ce pas, c'est un . . . état de
choses . . . c'est évident et Lahore, . . . Lahore, qu'est-ce que ça veut
dire?" (*VC* 42). (In this case, there is no plaintiff, do you see, it's
a . . . situation . . . that's obvious, and Lahore . . . who cares about Lahore? [E 29].)

Lahore and the vice-consul are *hors de la ville,* extramural. The law
of the polis, of the city-state, writes Hannah Arendt in *The Human
Condition,* was quite literally a wall without which there would be no
city, no political community. The law was identified with the boundary
line (63). Outside the pale, the vice-consul's crimes are not recognized.
He is like the beggars and the lepers, *hors caste*—a pariah. Perhaps he is
not quite like them, however. They are confused with dogs: "Mais de
lépreux ou des chiens, est-ce tuer que tuer des lépreux ou des chiens?"
(*VC* 94). (Lepers and dogs! Is it killing when it's merely the killing of
lepers and dogs?) *He* is merely "a little dead" ("un peu mort" [100]) while
he lives among other whites in the foreign service doing irreproachable
work, dressing impeccably, and looking even handsome were it not that

his face seemed empty, a blank ("il n'a pas de regard [*VC* 132]). He is marked as not the same, as *hors,* and his name inscribes it, marks it: *j'en marque*—Jean-Marc de H is the vice-consul's name. *H,* his patronymic, is only a single letter, but a telling one—its insistence in the text is the insistence of an absence, a loss—a letter that according to Lacan's prescription, I take literally (keeping in mind that what is literal is always already metaphorical). *H* in French pronounces the homonyms *ache,* a plant of the umbelliferous family; *hache,* "axe"; and its own name, which is silent or aspirate.

The aspirate *h* in French is the letter of separation.[3] It prevents any elision or liaison with the preceeding word. Although it does not make a full sound, in a breathless way it cuts a path, *un écart,* into the name Lahore and into the text. Its trace is heard in the echo of the gun shots in the Shalimar Gardens and in the wheezing of the asthmatic vice-consul himself, who, out of breath, must take to his balcony in the early mornings to breathe more easily. His wheezing and whistling (of "Indiana's Song"—"all he knew about India, until he came here" [E 116]) announce him, warn of his presence, seen or unseen, and linger in his absence. Lingering also in this sound/unsound of the text is the trace of the asthmatic Proust—the scratch of his distant pen. The vice-consul's labored breath is more of a calling card than his voice, which seems to belong to someone else. It is a "toneless voice" (E 87), "une voix ingrate comme greffée" (an unpleasant voice as if grafted onto him [*VC* 131]). He is the *greffe,* the graft, the grapheme, of the colonial intervention—the foreign edifice that sits on the festering, starving India.[4] The insistence of the name, of the letter, traces the boundary line of separation. Jean-Marc de H, always outside, does not belong anywhere, not in his native France, not in India, not in *le beau monde* of colonial Calcutta. He marks, is the mark of, the pariah par excellence.

Ache (spelled without an initial *h*) blends and pales phonetically in comparison to its homophonic counterpart, *hache,* whose *h* is aspirate. The definition of *ache* underwrites this and is yet another testament to the onomastic skill that Duras displays here and in other texts. The *Petit Robert* defines *ache* as "plante ombellifère, herbacée, dont espèces sont cultivées comme alimentaires, le céleri à côtes [celery] et le céleri-rave [celeriac]." Celery is generally blanched (*blanchir*) when grown, that is, tied up or otherwise kept from the sun so that its inner stalks and leaves (hearts of celery) are nearly devoid of color—an apt description of Jean-Marc de H. It is repeatedly remarked that he is deathly pale. Colorless-

ness prevails. Anne-Marie Stretter, too, is "pale under her Calcutta tan,
like all the other whites" (E 82). Charles Rossett finds it difficult to get
used to the heat, the monotony, and "the light, that colorless light"
("cette lumière, il n'y a aucune couleur" [*VC* 101]). Most of the women
have the pale skin of recluses, because they live behind closed shutters
that shelter them from the deadly sun ("le soleil-qui-tue" [100]).

Plants like *ache* that need protection from the sun are called umbelliferous (*ombellifère*) because of the umbels (*ombelles*) they bear—flat-topped
or rounded flower clusters emerging in a parasol shape from a common
center. In both French and English, the etymology is the same, both are
derived from *umbrella* and from *umbra;* in French the word is *ombre,*
shadow. Jean-Marc de H is a shadow man. He is an unsettling figure,
"un élément d'inquiétude," as *Petit Robert* defines *ombre*—the trace of a
disturbance that exploded into the violence of Lahore and the passion for
Anne-Marie Stretter. She sees him as "une image classique . . . une catastrophe [qui] peut éclater en un lieu lointain de celui où elle aurait dû se
produire" (a classical image . . . a catastrophe that can explode in a place
far from where it was produced [*VC* 129]). The distant place is France,
whose newest addition to the diplomatic corps in Calcutta is Charles
Rossett, to whom the doors of elite French society are thrown open.
The vice-consul of Lahore, however, obscure and secretive, has no ca-
chet. Although invited to official functions, he is nonetheless *hors des*
"cercles fermés aux Indes" (outside the inner circles of India [*VC* 103]).
In an old usage in English, the word *umbra* refers to an uninvited guest
who accompanies an invited one (*OED*). Jean-Marc de H is Charles
Rossett's umbra. He not only lives in his shadow but is a shadow, that
dark stain in Charles Rossett's brush with French colonial life in India.

Fresh from France in the years before World War II, Charles Rossett
is the fair-haired boy, ruddy and rosy, as his name says. He embodies
the promise of the future, but he also brings with him a tinge of the past.
His name carries in it the suggestion of Proust and *A la recherche de temps
perdu.* His first name evokes the figure of Charles Swann, who is red-
haired, and his last emphasizes that tint—red, *roux,* related to and so like
the English word *russet,* which is also red. Proust, read in Charles Rossett's name, is the *roux* that thickens the surface of Duras's text, that
binds the tissue of social relations of that moribund stratum of French
society to the unspeakable misery that is India, to France in India, where
its death rattle is heard.

Except for the red sky over the Indian Ocean at sunset, India has little color that the colonists can see. The vice-consul has the pallor of a specter, and Anne-Marie Stretter dresses only in black and white. The bit of color in the book is rose, the Proustian color of lost memories, of love and time lost, that washes the dream images that appear to Charles Rossett and Jean-Marc de H. One image occurs early in the book: "Nous avons rêvé d'un femme rose, rose liseuse rose qui lirait Proust dans le vent acide d'une Manche lointain" (*VC* 47). (We dreamt about a rosy woman, a rosily clad rosy reader who would read Proust in the bitter wind of a distant Channel.) The other image occurs at the book's end: "Elle lirait pendant ses couches, rose liseuse aux joues roses, Proust" (*VC* 211). (During her confinement, she, rosily clad rosy-cheeked reader, would read Proust.) Between the two citations is the story, *l'histoire,* the writing into which Duras loses herself.

The first sentence (and paragraph) of the novel tells of a writer writing: "Elle marche, écrit Peter Morgan" (*VC* 9). (She is walking, writes Peter Morgan.) Impossible to render in the English translation is the ambiguity of the pronoun *elle,* which can refer to both woman and story, *l'histoire,* whose gender is feminine. The same sentence could be read "It [the story] starts, writes Peter Morgan." The lines that follow are at once the instructions for the beggar woman's unwilling march into exile and a description, a map of sorts, of the mysterious trip—a willing exile—that writing is for Duras.

Elle marche, écrit Peter Morgan.

Comment ne pas revenir? Il faut se perdre. Je ne sais pas. Tu apprendras. Je voudrais une indication pour me perdre. Il faut être sans arrière-pensée, se disposer à ne plus reconnaître rien de ce qu'on connait, diriger ses pas vers le point de l'horizon le plus hostile, sorte de vaste étendu de marécages que mille talus traversent en tous sens on ne voit pourquoi. (*VC* 9)

(She is walking, writes Peter Morgan.

How to avoid going back? You have to get lost. I don't know how. You will learn. I would like some directions in order to get lost. You must not have any reservations. You must be ready to no longer recognize anything you know. You must direct your steps toward the most hostile point of the horizon, a kind of vast stretch of marshland crossed by a thousand causeways in every direction, without any reason.)

There are few signposts in Duras's texts, and those that exist may be unreliable. There is only movement, the movement of desire along the chain of signifiers, until her India, *son histoire,* and its stories of love and death are discovered. Like the word *histoire,* Duras's works reside in the interplay of story and history.

The opening passage above indicates the sense in which Duras avows that she remains unable to understand how she writes: "Quand je les relis [ses textes comme *Le vice-consul*], je suis étonné, je me dis: 'Qu'est-ce qui m'arrive?' Je ne comprend pas très bien. C'est comme ça, écrire" (*DM* 23). (When I reread them [her texts like *The Vice-Consul*], I'm astonished. I say to myself, "What's happening to me?" I don't understand very well. That's how it is, writing.) She knows, however, that she does not go through it alone.

> On écrit jamais seul . . . on écrit avec des gens qui nous ont précédés. Moi, j'écris avec Diderot, j'en suis sûre, avec Pascal, avec les grands hommes de ma vie, avec Kierkegaard, avec Rousseau . . . mais totalement à mon insu, c'est ma première nourriture que je lis avec avidité. (*DM* 23).

> (We never write alone. We write with those people who preceeded us. As for me, I write with Diderot, I'm sure of it, with Pascal, with the great men in my life, with Kierkegaard, with Rousseau . . . but completely without my knowing it; it is my first food that I read greedily.)

She does not mention Proust among these predecessors—an omission that may be a manifestation of her "anxiety of influence," to invoke Harold Bloom's theory. Perhaps those who are most with her are the ones she omits. The unconscious, so close to (the) writing, plays its tricks. This possibility causes her to see herself as no more a privileged reader of her texts than the rest of us.

An extended description of the delta rice fields and the causeways through which Anne-Marie Stretter, Charles Rossett, and Michael Richard drive on their way to the islands is, despite its different emphasis and tone, redolent of Proust's lines on the streets of Venice, a city of waterways.

Immense étendu de marécages que mille talus traversent en tous
sens. . . . On est dans un pays d'eau, à la frontière entre les eaux et
les eaux, douces, salées, qui dans les baies se mélangent déjà avec la
glace verte de l'océan. (*VC* 175–76)

(An immense stretch of marshland crossed by a thousand causeways
crossing in all directions. . . . We are in a watery land, at the border-
line separating the waters, fresh and salt, black, that in the bays are
already mixed with the icy green of the ocean.)

Comprimées les unes contre les autres, ces calli divisaient en tous
sens, de leurs rainures, le morceau de Venise découpé entre un canal
et la lagune, comme s'il avait cristallisé suivant ces formes innom-
brables, ténues et minutieuses. (Proust 3:650–51)

(I had plunged into a network of little alleys, or *calli,* packed tightly
together and dissecting in all directions with their furrows a chink
of Venice carved out between a canal and lagoon, as if it had crystal-
lized in accordance with these innumerable, tenuous and minute
patterns. (K 3:665)[5]

Anne-Marie Stretter, who at official functions had "the look of an
exile" (*VC* 92), lived in Venice and played the piano there when she was
Anna Maria Guardi. The name Guardi is synonymous with Venice for
those who know those eighteenth-century paintings of that city done
by one of its foremost *vedutisti,* Francesco Guardi (Wittkower 503–5).
His scenes of shimmering canals and lagoons lapping against the streets
and splendid buildings of Venice are part of Marcel's memory of that
city (Proust 3:710) and perhaps part of Duras's memory, too, of her avid
reading and her struggles in a watery exile so evident in *L'amant.* Proust
always describes one woman's face and complexion with some reference
to roses, the color or the flower, "tiges de roses dont le principal charme
de se détacher sur la mer" (rose sprigs whose principle charm was that
they were silhouetted against the sea [1:944; K 1:1007]). He writes, "Elle
était non pas fraîche, mais lisse d'un rose uni, violacé, cremeux, comme
certain roses qui ont un vernis de cire" (She was not fresh and cool but
smooth, with a uniform pinkness, violet-tinted, creamy, like certain

roses whose petals have a waxy gloss [1:888; K 1:949]). The woman,
who, like Anne-Marie Stretter, "seemed to be feeling the sorrows of
exile" (elle semblait éprouver une tristesse d'exilée [K 1:1009; 1:946]), is
Albertine, a rosy-cheeked cyclist from Balbec by the sea, for whom
Marcel has so obsessive a passion that it keeps him from satisfying his
other intense desire—to see Venice.

The wishes, fantasies, dreams, and memories of the characters, the
writer, and the reader, and the relation among them all are strung together by a thread of language that Duras weaves into a text (an idea
adduced by Freud in "The Relation of the Poet to Daydreaming" [44–
45]). Throughout the novel are various attitudes of reading and writing.
Peter Morgan writes about the mad beggar woman. The vice-consul
reads his aunt's letter, rereads some passages, and announces: "Elle a été
lue" (*VC* 33). (It [she] has been read). Charles Rossett reads the vice-
consul's dossier. The vice-consul's childhood room smells of blotting
paper and erasers. And while dreamers dream of "une rose liseuse,"
readers see not only that "rosy reader," but *une rose liseuse,* a rose-colored
bedjacket, a garment designed to keep one warm while sitting up in bed
reading, and a rose-colored bookcover, sometimes made of leather, also
une rose liseuse; the reader sees the trappings—the signifiers—of reading.
Proust in *Le vice-consul* has become the condition of reading (two references in the book to reading Proust are in the conditional tense), and
Albertine, the prototype of the "rosy reader," marks the page, is *un
signet,* a bookmark, more precisely, *une liseuse,* a bookmark with a knife
edge for cutting open the pages of a book so that it may be read, the sign
(*signe*[t]) that the book has been read.

In Duras's text, the Albertine figure, the rosy "prisonnière," is the
floating signifier of that which cannot be possessed: lovers and India.
Proust writes: "On aime que ce qu'on ne possede pas et bien vite je
remettais à me rendre compte que je ne possédais pas Albertine" (3:384).
("One only loves what one does not possess, and very soon I began to
realise once more that I did not possess Albertine" [K 3:391].) *The Romance of the Rose* persists. "Une femme rose, rose liseuse rose qui lirait
Proust" is about the desire for the rose that is not there, and Duras knows
that. As Gertrude Stein said: "It's doubly hard to be a poet in a late
age. . . . [In] hundreds of poems about roses . . . you know in your bones
that the rose is not there" (*Look at Me Now* 7). So when she said, "a rose
is a rose is a rose," it was not a joke, it was "re[a]d for the first time in
English poetry for a hundred years" (*Look at Me Now* 7). In Duras's line,

the desire for the rose circulates and ends (up) in Proust, a tome of desire. In the story, Anne-Marie Stretter signals the end of the dance by distributing roses to her women guests—"elle n'aime pas beaucoup les fleurs" (she doesn't like flowers very much [*VC* 140]). Proust has been read in and by Duras.

Anne-Marie Stretter is the shadowy, disconcerting figure in Charles Rossett's rosy dream, where he sees her dressed in white shorts crossing the deserted tennis courts. Half in love with her, he has delayed asking to be transferred from Calcutta, to whose crushing heat and poverty he seems unable to adjust. Succumbing to his passion for her will bring him into her court, where, like others before him, he will become inured, habituated to the daily outrage that passes for existence there. Not unlike the ladies of high estate in earlier centuries who sat above the din of the quotidian and created courts of *politesse* and *courtoisie,* Anne-Marie Stretter will become the source of his "tranquillité d'esprit" (peace of mind [*VC* 195]). She will play the piano for him and make love to him through the tears of her ineffable sadness. His life will come to resemble hers, which she describes as "ni facile, ni difficile, ce n'est rien" (neither easy nor difficult, it's nothing [*VC* 109]). Emblematic perhaps of this vapid life are the deserted tennis courts. Against the wire fence that encloses them is her bicycle, left out, as if forgotten. The image of the lone bicycle is suffused with nostalgia. A remnant waiting for the rest to appear, it is unfailingly evocative and can cause the imagination to unreel stories of past possibilities. It is an ultra Proustian image (Albertine's bicycle is abandoned when she becomes Marcel's "captive") of ennui, desire, and absence. For the vice-consul of Lahore, it becomes the representative for its absent rider, a synecdoche; a part for the whole. His love for Anne-Marie Stretter remains *hors sexe* (outside sex).

Inspired by Guy de Maupassant's strange coinage of the word *Horla,* Lacan invented the neologism *Horsexe* to indicate the possibility that love may consist in something other than the sexual relation (Mitchell and Rose 155). Not only is *Horsexe* applicable to Jean-Marc de H, who is still a virgin, but *Horla* recalls the name Lahore in a reversal of its syllables. Phonically, the reversal is perfect; orthographically, the silent *e* is dropped. As if the link here between chance and necessity is not clear enough, the word *Horla* phonically means "outside it"—precisely where the vice-consul remains.

Although it is not certain what the *Horla* is, a 1911 English translation of the tale adds an interesting subtitle to the original, rendering it

as "the Horla or Modern Ghosts" (Maupassant, McMaster's trans. 4:1).
It is reasonable to assume that the *Horla* is some sort of psychic phe-
nomenon that evokes a sense of otherness, madness, and augurs death
by, among other things, preventing the protagonist of the story from
seeing his reflection in the mirror. As he stares horrified at the empty
mirror, a mist rises from its depths, travels across it slowly, then, as at
the end of an eclipse, allows the mirror its proper reflections once more.
He has become so distraught by this that in an effort to trap and kill the
Horla, he sets his house on fire, killing his servants in it (Maupassant
446–49). Silent echoes of Lahore, of shattered mirrors and death in the
Shalimar Gardens, linger in our reading of this bizarre tale, in which
there is, speaking generally, a rereading of Freud. Maupassant knew
Mesmer's work on hypnosis (featured in the tale *Horla*) and Charcot's
in La Salpêtrière on hysteria (Maupassant 431–35, 562 n. 8), both
significant in Freud's early development. Duras is conversant with
Freud, but not with Lacan, who said of her when he read *Le ravissement
of Lol V. Stein:* "She knows, without me, what I teach" ("Hommage"
124). He recognizes her subject, like his, to be the unconscious—the
subject she shares with Maupassant.[6]

The vice-consul of Lahore, fixed in the *Horsexe,* "makes love" to
Anne-Marie Stretter's bicycle in a delicately described scene that Charles
Rossett sees from a distance.

> Le vice-consul quitte l'allée et s'approche de la bicyclette.
> Il fait quelque chose. A cette distance il est difficile de savoir
> exactement quoi. Il a l'air de la regarder, de la toucher, il se penche
> sur elle longuement, il se redresse, la regarde encore.
> Il revient dans l'allée et repart un peu titubant mais d'un pas
> tranquille. . . .
> La bicyclette contre la grillage est récouverte de la fine poussière
> grise de l'allée.
> Elle est abandonnée, sans emploi, effrayante. . . .
> Quelqu'un, au loin, sifflote *Indiana's Song.* On ne voit pas qui.
> (*VC* 49–50)

> (The vice-consul leaves the path and approaches the bicycle.
> He is doing something. From this distance it is difficult to know
> exactly what. He seems to be looking at it, touching it. He bends
> over it for a long time. He straightens up and looks at it again.

He returns to the path and starts off again, staggering a bit, but
with an even step. . . .
The bicycle against the wire fence is covered with a fine gray dust
from the path.
It is abandoned, unused, frightening. . . .
Someone in the distance whistles "Indiana's Song." You can't tell
who.)

At the wire fence of the deserted tennis court, an act that Duras calls
"solitaire, obscur, abominable" (VC 103) is also one of adoration of the
seat of love—not only a risqué *jeu de mots,* but an instance of synecdochic
substitution. The ministry of passion is Anne-Marie Stretter's. She is the
seat of love in the inner circles, in a debased version of a tradition that
began with the Provençal troubadours at the end of the eleventh century,
that of courtly love.

Lacan points out that "courtly love is the only way of coming off
elegantly from the absence of sexual relation . . . [and is] rooted in the
discourse of fealty, of fidelity to the person. In the last resort, the person
is always the discourse of the master" (Mitchell and Rose 141). According to C. S. Lewis: "The lover is the lady's 'man.' He addresses her as
midons, which etymologically represents not 'my lady' but 'my lord.'"
The lady (always a married lady) is in charge, and the reward for perfect
fealty is carnal knowledge (2, 12–15). For the vice-consul's devotion to
Anne-Marie Stretter, no reward awaits him, no promise of carnal
knowledge. Rather, they share a perfect intimacy in the unspoken
knowledge of the carnage that is Lahore. Their union is sealed by other
means. In what could be seen as an instance of peripeteia, he learns that
she has kept their intimacy intact by lying for him. Charles Rossett says
to the vice-consul, "Il parait que vous avez peur de la lèpre?" (You're
afraid of leprosy, it seems?) The remark infuriates him. "C'est un men-
songe. Qui a parle de ça?" (It's a lie. Who told you that?) "Madame
Stretter," answers Rossett. "Brutalement la colère du vice-consul le
quitte, et une pensée lui vient qui l'inonde comme ferait le bonheur" (VC
139). (Abruptly, the vice-consul's anger leaves him, and a thought comes
over him, saturating him as happiness would.)

To lie in the name of troth (a variation of truth meaning loyalty,
allegiance) is a vertiginous instance of irony that parallels the abrupt
reversal of the vice-consul's state of mind. In a footnote to H. S.
Butcher's commentary on Aristotle's notion of peripeteia, there is a

remarkable formulation in which just such a parallel is indicated: "περιπέτεια is to actions what irony is to language." Though this does not
apply to every instance of peripeteia, "an overruled intention, with new
significance thereby added to the event, is one of the special forms which
περιπέτεια may assume. It is worth observing that περιπετεῖα so
modified sometimes approaches nearly to what is known in modern
criticism as the 'Irony of Destiny'" (Butcher 331). Kenneth Burke writes
of irony that "as an overall formula . . . , one that has the quality of
'inevitability,' we could lay it down that 'what goes forth as A returns
as non-A'" (517). The inevitability of Lahore brings the Vice-Consul the
only love of his life. Anne-Marie Stretter will not betray their secret
knowledge. In a travesty of the rite, she plights her troth to him with a
lie—for him a significant turn of events.

Ironically, Charles Rossett, to whom Anne-Marie Stretter *has*
opened her arms, wants to share just such a binding knowledge with
her. During an embrace, he says: "'Nous ne nous connaissons pas, dite-
moi quelque chose . . . Je ne sais pas pourquoi . . . Je vous en supplie . . .'
Elle ne dit rien" (*VC* 190). ("We don't know anything about each other,
tell me something . . . I don't know why . . . I beg of you . . . " She says
nothing.) With Rossett, her love must remain an instrument of silent
oblivion, of knowing nothing. Because the vice-consul is a reflection of
what he knows, a knowledge in which she is complicit, she cannot allow
him into her arms or her circle. The look of someone other that is seen
in his face is death—the *Horla* perhaps. His is the white face of the
"clown" (*VC* 127) who plays (with) death. If she relents, the inner circles
of India will give way to India itself. Charles Rossett, who recognizes
her instrumentality, her passivity, who recognizes her finally as "La
Whore," loses his desire for her, while the vice-consul remains her loyal
vassal and does her bidding. He shrieks—cries out for his impossible
love and for Lahore.

Although steadfast, the vice-consul, a miserable and debased figure,
has hardly the grandeur of the knight, hardly the brilliance of Lancelot,
for example, the hero of Chrétien de Troyes's masterpiece that was the
"flowering of the courtly tradition in France" (C. S. Lewis 23). He is a
stand-in for the knight, as his title *vice*-consul suggests. He is like the
squire who runs with the knight carrying his shield, a figure described
by Gregor von Rezzori in "Troth," one of his *Memoirs of an Anti-Semite,*
in which he points out that intimate commerce with Jews was even

"worse than treason and breach of troth; it was *the* incomprehensible" (205).

It is a great irony that the word for squire, the German *neb-ich* (near-I) is preserved only in the Yiddish (mainly Middle High German with Hebrew and Polish elements) expression *nebbish* (Rezzori 207). The nebbish is generally understood today as a person who really does not manage very well in the world for one reason or another, no matter how hard he or she tries—often the harder the person tries, the worse he or she fares. The nebbish is kin to the schlemiel, a Jewish folk figure who also survives as a Yiddish expression. According to Hannah Arendt in "The Jew as Pariah: the Hidden Tradition," the character of the schlemiel was drawn by the German Jewish poet Heinrich Heine in his poem *Princess Sabbath* (69). Arendt relates Heine's story of how the term *schlemiel* evolved from the name of Shelumiel ben Zurishaddai, who is mentioned in the Book of Numbers as a leader of the tribe of Simeon. Because Herr Shelumiel ben Zurishaddai was standing too close to his brother, the chieftain Zimri, he got himself killed accidentally when Zimri was beheaded by the priest Phinehas for dallying with a Midianite woman (Arendt, "JP" 70).

"Innocence is the hallmark of the schlemiel. But it is of such innocence that a people's poets—its 'lords of dreams'—are born," writes Arendt. She also reminds us that if the lords of dreams—the schlemiels—"may claim Shelumiel as their ancestor, they must also claim the ruthless Phinehas," who did the killing" ("JP" 70). The tradition of the schlemiel is not one of purity or unerring behavior. Although not without blemish, the vice-consul is an innocent of sorts and, in effect, a pariah, who is in the unlikely position of having been sent to govern a country that has a rigid caste system, the lowest of whom are of course called pariahs. Such is the typical arrangement of circumstances that often befalls the schlemiel. The cosmic roar of laughter can be heard in the inevitability of (what happened that night in) Lahore.

The vice-consul is first cousin to the schlemiel. He is as remote and unreal to the world of society as it is to him, and he stands outside it. Although he wants to get in, he cannot manage to ingratiate himself enough to do so. Anne-Marie Stretter keeps him on the outside, a nowhere, where he belongs. She knows that "il n'a pas besoin de rien" (he doesn't need anything [*VC* 155]) and especially that "il n'a pas besoin de moi" (he doesn't need me [*VC* 192]). Perhaps in this knowledge the hand of Duras can be discerned. Something of a pariah herself, having been born a colonial without means, Duras, like Heine, is saved by her creativity, by her writing, from lapsing into utopianism. She is thus enabled, to use Arendt's words about Heine, "to transform the political non-existence and unreality of the pariah into the effective basis of a world of art" ("Jew as Pariah" 73).

The vice-consul, reassigned to Bombay, remains, as it were, the schlemiel—the dreamer—who dreams (a dream redolent, perhaps, of blotting paper and erasers) that his aunt finds him a silly little white goose of a wife from Neuilly, whose name will be Nicole Courseules (*VC* 211)—an empty, solitary name. The umbrageous vice-consul tells the director of the club about his rosy, Rossett dream: "Elle lirait dans ses couches, rose liseuse rose aux joues roses, Proust" (*VC* 211). (During her confinement, she, rosily clad rosy-cheeked reader would read Proust.) Of Proust, who was half-Jewish and homosexual, Arendt writes in *Antisemitism,* the first part of the *Origins of Totalitarianism:* "the question [before him] is not as for Hamlet, to be or not to be, but to belong or not to belong" (84). The vice-consul, who does not belong, will look into the eyes of his "rose liseuse," who he dreams belongs to him, and will see the look of terror. "On n'aime que ce en quoi on poursuit quelque chose d'inaccessible" (Proust 3:384). ("One only loves that in which one pursues the inaccessible" [K 3:391].) "L'aimez-vous?" (Do you love her?) asks the director. "Parlez-moi des Iles, directeur" (*VC* 211). The vice-consul answers him by asking to hear once more about the islands and about the Prince of Wales, the favorite hotel there of Anne-Marie Stretter and her circle.

The distance between the vice-consul and the schlemiel, that is, between the French colonial agency in India in the thirties and the Jewish Question, is bridged by Duras's experience.

> Je crois que les juifs, ce trouble pour moi si fort . . . a une fonction de regroupment de l'horreur latente répandue sur le monde, et que je reconnais. . . . Le mot juif dit en même temps la puissance de mort que l'homme peut s'octroyer et sa reconnaisance par nous. C'est parce que les nazis n'ont pas *reconnu* cette horreur en eux qu'ils l'ont commise. Les juifs, ce trouble, *ce déjà vu,* a du certainement commencer—pour moi—avec l'enfance en Asie, les lazarets hors des villages, l'endémie de la peste, du choléra, de la misère, les rue

condamnées des pestiférées sont les premiers camps de concentration que j'ai vus. (*YV* 86)

(I believe that the Jews, that disorder that troubles me so profoundly, acts as a concentration of that horror that is latent all over the world and that I recognize. The word *Jew* stands alone in the death-dealing power that man may arrogate to himself and our recognition of that power. It's because the Nazis did not recognize, did not acknowledge this horror within themselves, that they acted as they did. That disorder that is the Jews, that déjà vu, must certainly have begun for me with my childhood in Asia. The leper colonies outside the villages, the endemic plagues of cholera, of poverty, and the off-limit streets of the plague-ridden were the first concentration camps I saw.

The memory of those early camps (and intimate knowledge of the effects of the later ones) reappear in the space of writing, in the rectangular space of the empty white page, as writing, as configurations of other empty spaces: in "les tennis déserts" (the deserted tennis courts) in *Le vice-consul,* in "le rectangle blanc de la cour de rassemblement du camp" (the white [blank] rectangle of the camp's assembly grounds) in "Aurélia Steiner," in "la cave à Nevers" (the cellar in Nevers) in *Hiroshima mon amour,* in the bed and the room across the river in *L'amant,* in *Maladie de la mort,* and in others—spaces of death and absence that contain stories of love. Duras maintains: "Mais l'écrit, lui, le texte, il passe par un filtre qui le transforme. Il passe par une transgression que j'appelle le filtre. Cette modification définitive du filtre, c'est l'écrit" (*DM* 58). (But the writing, the text itself, passes through a filter that transforms it. It passes through a transgression that I call the filter. That definitive modification of the filter, is the writing.) The space of experience, of forgetting, of blank pages, is filled letter by letter with the words that in their insistence, their repetition, become "une sorte de désincrustation de l'expérience et même de l'imaginaire" (a kind of unloosening of experience and even of the imaginary [*DM* 58]) and signify on the page those haunting absences that, like the *Horla* in the mirror, flicker like Lahore in the eyes of the vice-consul.

Chapter 4

Hannah Arendt

All sorrows can be borne if you put them into a story or tell a story about them.

—Isak Dinesen

Sense how the purest story
Still hides everything.

—Hannah Arendt, from an early poem

Hannah Arendt's writings have always had a maverick, marginal, and even experimental tinge to them—a tinge that has recently sparked new interest in her among some intellectuals in Paris who are trying to integrate the human sciences according to a new paradigm (Dupuy 19). What they find so interesting about her is that her writings work along the borders of several disciplines. That Arendt's work is so difficult to categorize is entirely consistent with her stance in the world. Her position does not emblazon itself in granite, is not systemized. She cannot be pigeonholed into a political position or type. It has been said of her, "It is never clear what, if anything, Miss Arendt is for or against" (Young-Bruehl 424), and, "How [can] such a conservative and such a radical . . . co-exist in one person, . . . there must be two Arendts" (Hill 22). When asked directly, "Are you a conservative? Are you a liberal? Where is your position within the contemporary possibilities?" she replied:

> I really don't know and I've never known. And I suppose I never had such a position. You know the left think I am conservative and the conservatives think I am left or I am a maverick or God knows what. And I must say I couldn't care less. I don't think the real

questions of this century will get any kind of illumination by this kind of thing. ("OHA" 333–34)

If Arendt has a method, it is simply that she responds to issues at hand and thinks them through against the background of her rich philosophical culture. As she says, "the subject of our thought . . . [is] experience. Nothing else. And if we lose the ground of experience then we get into all kinds of theories" ("AA" 308). Arendt thinks of these theories as great fictions and eschews the system building of political theorists and philosophers because the work becomes far too abstract and often causes theorists to turn away from the work itself. This abstraction can lead to false estimations of things as they are, a situation Arendt lived through in Germany when the Nazis were gaining power. Some of her colleagues and teachers, Jewish and Gentile, could not, or would not, stop their work to see and understand what was developing around them.[1] Arendt did stop, however, and turned to politics, as did, years before her, Rosa Luxemburg, a martyr to socialist struggles, a heroine to Martha Arendt, Hannah's mother, and a thinker and activist whose work Arendt knew and came to appreciate. Luxemburg gave up her intellectual concerns to turn to politics because, as Arendt wrote of her, "circumstances of the world offended her sense of justice and freedom" (*MDT* 38).

In the late twenties and early thirties, Arendt was not at all politically oriented. She had just completed a dissertation on "The Concept of Love in Augustine" and was already at work on some writers and thinkers of the German Romantic period when she felt she had to reconsider her life in Germany, not just as a philosopher and intellectual, but as a Jew living in an increasingly hostile environment. Like Luxemburg, the circumstances of the world around her had begun "to offend her sense of justice and freedom." She opened her eyes to the Jewish Question for the first time and began to study, to engage in a thinking through of an issue at hand. This is what eventually culminated in her first large political work, the tripartite *Origins of Totalitarianism,* the first part of which is called *Antisemitism.* Her way toward that work spanned the eighteen years of her exile. She fled Germany without papers in 1933 after her arrest and eight-day detainment, and she spent the next eight years, stateless, in Paris. After Paris fell, she escaped from an internment camp in Vichy France near the Spanish border in 1941 and emigrated again, this time to the United States, where ten years later she finally became a citizen. Much of the basis for *Antisemitism* and for some of *Imperialism,* part two of *Origins,* which includes an impassioned chapter on being stateless, can be found in her biography *Rahel Varnhagen: The Life of a Jewess,* which she wrote in 1932–33 (except for the last two chapters, which she completed in Paris in 1938).

This biography of Rahel (as Rahel Antonie Fredericke Varnhagen von Ense, née Levin, came to be called in German letters) is unusual on many counts. It is ostensibly a biography of a prodigious letter writer, an important cultural figure whose writing reveals a good deal of the bourgeois social texture of the late eighteenth and early nineteenth centuries, and who initiated the Goethe cult and held one of those illustrious salons frequented by Schlegel, Schleiermacher, and other leading German Romantics. It is as much (and perhaps more) about the individual and the world (in today's parlance, the microcosmic and macrocosmic views). It is about what is worldless and worldly, about pariahs (the marginal) and parvenus (the assimilated), and about the condition of Jews in Germany 150 years ago. It is about all these relations as Arendt came to understand them by examining the life's thought of this individual Jewish woman as it appeared in her unpublished diaries and in her letters, both published and not (*RV* xiii–xiv). It is Arendt's penetrating insight that Rahel sought to find not so much her self but the world and her legitimate place in it—precisely what Arendt was doing at the time of the writing.

The book is Arendt's thinking through of an issue at hand, and it resulted in a writing that is as much her autobiography as it is Rahel's biography. It is not a strict recounting of occurrences, of places and people (the chronology of Rahel's life appears mainly as dates in parentheses below the chapter headings), nor the concrete details that attempt to explain the hows and whys of a subject's life (the various persons in the book are discussed only from Rahel's point of view [*RV* xvii]). It is a narrative that constitutes Arendt's sustained meditation, which in this case is about Rahel's lifelong development toward her deathbed declaration that "the thing which all my life seemed to me the greatest shame, which was the misery and misfortune of my life—having been born a Jewess—this I should on no account now wish to have missed" (*RV* 3).

The book is a type of bildungsroman in which Arendt shows how Rahel went from being intensely introspective, bordering on the solipsistic, to recognizing her desire for the world, for being in the world. She does this by reading Rahel through her own developing historical consciousness of German Jews from the Enlightenment and the great period of assimilation to the time of the writing of *Rahel Varnhagen,* when the impending doom of the Jews was on the horizon. This realization under-writes the text (*RV* xvii). As she is careful to point out in her preface to the English version published in 1957, Arendt did not know at the time she wrote the book, that the history of the Jews in Germany would soon come to a final end. How exquisitely poignant, though, is that develop-ing consciousness for readers after the fact of the annihilation of German Jewry.

The forcible ending of a history of a large and thriving group of people is so cataclysmic that it takes Arendt's writing on Rahel, which is now part of that history, out of the realm of the ordinary: "The German-speaking Jews and their history are an altogether unique phe-nomenon; nothing comparable to it is to be found even in other areas of Jewish assimilation" (*RV* xvii). Recall Marguerite Duras's writing of her screenplay about Hiroshima, the scene of another catastrophic event in World War II (p. 71). Duras explains: "Nothing is 'given' in Hiroshima. Every gesture, every word takes on an aura of meaning that transcends its literal meaning" (*Hiroshima Mon Amour* 9). The irrevocable knowl-edge of such events by post-1945 readers makes such works as *Rahel Varnhagen* and *Hiroshima mon amour* not only cautionary but paradig-matic. Rahel's (re)conversion to her own birthright is a tragic and stun-ning victory—irredeemably human, the stamp of which is found in the plurality of stories that are part of history, that "great story without beginning or end" (Arendt, *HC* 184). For Arendt "putting the story into shape is a form of thought" that must bring understanding, and recon-ciliation—a recognition of things as they are. This is of paramount im-portance to Arendt: "I cannot live without trying at least to understand whatever happens" ("OHA" 303). These issues of thought and reconcili-ation have to do with recollection, remembrance, and complement Du-ras's notion of forgetting and remembering that is so much a part of her poiesis, her way of writing.

In the preface to *Rahel Varnhagen,* Arendt claims that although "there is always a certain awkwardness in an author speaking of his book, even one written half a lifetime ago," she will "nevertheless ven-ture a few explanatory remarks" because the "book was conceived and written from an angle unusual in biographical literature" (*RV* xv). Ar-endt explains that it was never her intention to write a book about Rahel, about her personality, or of the things she accomplished or influenced, which might lend itself to various interpretations according to the psychological standards and categories the author introduces from the outside. What interested me solely was *to narrate the story of Rahel's life as she herself might have told it.* (*RV* xv; my emphasis)

Although Arendt "naturally" uses "different language"—these are her words—she insists that her "portrait follows . . . as closely as possible the course of Rahel's own reflections" (*RV* xvi). She was justifiably skeptical about intentions: "I may not always carry them out successfully and at such times may appear to be passing judgment upon Rahel from some higher vantage point. If so, I have simply failed in what I have set out to do" (*RV* xvii).

It is hard to gauge how successful Arendt was in her endeavor. She undoubtedly achieved part of her goal, a certain portrait of Rahel. According to a 1958 review of the biography by the English writer Sybille Bedford, Arendt "seems to have succeeded" in what she set out to do. Of Rahel's verbalizations of her own reactions and feelings, Bedford writes:

> Miss Arendt is content to adumbrate and amplify. Reflection caps reflection, comment encompasses comment, and precedes event; the factual bones lie muffled in paragraphs of words like coins inside a ball of knitting wool. Miss Arendt does not break the subject's mood; [she is] faithful to her original conceptions. ("Emancipation and Destiny" 22)

But whether Arendt told this story as Rahel would have is arguable and probably undecidable. In the end, it is unlikely, as even Arendt came to see.

Some ten years after she wrote the preface to the English *Rahel Varnhagen,* in a review of Parmenia Miguel's biography of Isak Dinesen, Arendt writes of the shortcomings of this biography and of Dinesen's great and foolish desire for it at the end of her life. She declares, "No one, obviously, could have told the story of her life as she herself might have told it" (*MDT* 99–100). In ten years, Arendt has done an apparent *volte face.* The statement could be a reference to Dinesen's formidable abilities, but it seems to me to be a realization on Arendt's part finally that one cannot write like someone else (deliberate parody aside)—not even "like a woman." Here I invoke Peggy Kamuf's essay, "Writing like a Woman," which rehearses the legitimacy/illegitimacy of authorship, the undecidability of its gender.

Writing is, from a theoretical point of view, in the domain of the masculine. As Kamuf puts it, "Using language, whether as poet or critic—we are all more or less, in the position of a father, the parent of mediation." One must try to figure out how to "write as a woman"—an endeavor that Kamuf conludes rarely leads beyond biological determinism ("Writing Like a Woman" 284). One cannot write as (as if one were) a generic woman, another individual woman, or even one's self. Arendt, explaining Heidegger on thinking, writes, "The thinking 'I' is everything but the self of consciousness" ("Martin Heidegger at Eighty" 298). This premise is also true of the writing "I": it is split and forever trying to catch up with itself, as Lacan argues (*Ecrits: A Selection* 2). *Wo Es war, soll Ich werden* is Freud's lapidary formulation. In *The Human Condition*, Arendt explains, "It is more than likely that the 'who' [who one is] which appears so clearly and unmistakenly to others remains hidden from the person himself" (179).

Writing is always more than, in excess of, intentions. What appears in the writing can be apprehended by an understanding of "the modern verb of the middle voice *to write*," in which "the subject is immediately contemporary with the writing, being effected and affected by it"—a conclusion drawn by Roland Barthes in his essay, "To Write: An Intransitive Verb?" (143). The essay ends with a telling investigation of voice (active, passive, and middle, the last now obsolete in modern Indo-European languages) in which he finds that the opposition is not between the active and passive voices but between the active and middle, and that in the middle voice, the subject affects itself in the acting, that it always remains inside the action (without excluding transitivity). Barthes sees that the middle voice "corresponds exactly to the state of the verb *to write*. [I]t is to effect writing in being affected oneself; it is to leave the writer [*scripteur*] inside the writing, not a psychological subject, . . . but as the agent of the action" (142).

In French, the verb *to write* in the *passé composé* (past perfect tense) is *j'ai écrit* (I wrote). Written in the middle voice, *I wrote* would become *je suis écrit* and would take its place as one of a number of verbs of activity that in French, oddly enough, take the passive auxiliary *être* (to be). The difference in the two voices is clearly felt in a literal English translation: *j'ai écrit* says in English, "I have written"; *je suis écrit* says, "I am written." Though transitivity is not excluded from the middle voice, the verb *to write* begins to take on an intransitive feeling. As Barthes puts it, "The writer . . . [is] no longer one who writes *something,* but who writes absolutely." He cites as an example the answer (given "at least in more or less intellectual circles") to the question "'What is he doing?'—'He's writing'" ("To Write" 141). The writing, then, is not simply a product of the author's but becomes "the field of the writer" (144), writer and writing (and field) being produced at the same time, and diminishing the distance between the writer and the language asymptotically (143).

This new understanding of writing is interestingly similar to Arendt's description of Heidegger's passionate thinking in her essay "Martin Heidegger at Eighty." This is a "thinking through" in which the passivity is removed by putting the thinker inside the action of thinking, thereby creating in this case a transitivity for the verb that it did not enjoy before. It becomes an entirely uncontemplative activity in which what is discovered or illuminated is not as important as the laying down of "pathways" and fixing of "'trail marks' (a collection of [Heidegger's] texts from the years 1929–1962 had the title, *Wegmarken*)." But Arendt writes that thinking

> always has something by which it is specifically aroused; . . . one cannot say that it has a goal. It is unceasingly active, and even the laying down of paths itself is conducive to opening up a new dimension of thought, rather than to reaching a goal sighted beforehand and guided thereto. ("Martin Heidegger at Eighty" 296)

With writing, the same condition exists: the writer is not anterior to the writing. The writer does not know what he or she is writing until he or she writes. This notion has a Heideggerian ring to it, of process, of unfolding, that calls to mind Plotinus's words, "We must seek the light we are seeking by means of the light we seek"—a simultaneity of existence and inquiry, just as there is, by substitution, a simultaneity of existence and thinking and existence and writing in all these ideas. Perhaps this ring sounded in Arendt's ears when she read Rahel's line, "Everyone has a Destiny who knows what kind of destiny he has" (*RV* xvi).

Arendt understands that Rahel "considered herself extraordinary, but her view of the source of that quality differed from others" (*RV* xv). Rahel's explanations of that source resided in "innumerable phrases and images" with which she sought "to formulate the meaning of what she called Destiny." "What am I doing? Nothing. I am letting life rain upon me," wrote Rahel (*RV* xvi). She became a mouthpiece for experience, verbalized whatever happened. She did not choose or act. She practiced an introspection in which she related her own story repeatedly to herself and others until that story, that relating became her destiny. But as Bedford points out, it was not factual information Rahel wrote but her reactions, her feelings. She wrote down her emotions. These verbalizations became her experiences. She lost the world and gained a self that depended on its "capacity for pain," its alertness and susceptibility to life as it struck her "'like a storm without an umbrella'" (*RV* xvi). Arendt responds to Rahel's responses, resulting in, as Bedford writes in her review, "a relentlessly abstract book—slow, cluttered, static, curiously oppressive; reading it feels like sitting in a hothouse with no watch" ("Emancipation and Destiny" 22–23).

Though Bedford's is an astute characterization of the feel of Arendt's book, she does not really make enough of what I think turns up the heat in the hothouse and gets rid of the watch—Arendt's palpable presence in the mediated milieu. Arendt has bypassed time and space by writing herself into the claustrophobic, fervid world of Rahel's "narrated emotions," by writing about that written world. The result is something like a triple tier of reactions and analyses—Rahel's, Arendt's, and the reader's—that works like an expandable telescope that when fully extended circumscribes the focus to bring the distance and the eye closer together. This is an aspect of Arendt's thinking based on Heidegger's "coming-into-nearness to the distant" ("Martin Heidegger at Eighty" 300), a clumsy locution at best, but one that serves to suggest the movement of thought that suspends time and space to effect understanding. The telescope, here a simile, is less obviously a metaphor for the middle-voiced writing and passionate thinking that puts the writing, thinking subject into process, into the text, and provides the distance for the perspective and the choice of focus. "Our power over things grows in proportion to our distance from them," writes Arendt in "The Archimedian Point" (6). The reader, furthest away of all, feels the hothouse and senses the loss of time when hearing the two voices together that are a hundred years apart. The subjecthood of the text, then, is problematized: the book is about Arendt as well as Rahel.

Arendt is analyst to Rahel, and the reader becomes one to Arendt. This kind of psychoanalysis, if we may call it that, is of a peculiar post-Freudian or French cast that has neither the pretensions of psycho-

biography nor the aim of forcing the subject's experience into preset
categories and complexes. In her preface, Arendt disclaims, shuns actually, any use in her text of "pseudo-scientific apparatuses of depth psychology, psychoanalysis, graphology, etc." She refuses such analytical
approaches because she does not want to "impose upon [Rahel] . . . a
fictional destiny derived from observation presumed to be superior to
those she consciously had." She is keeping a sensible distance by "avoid-
ing that modern form of indiscretion in which the writer attempts to
know more than the subject knew about himself or was willing to reveal" (*RV* xviii). Yet Arendt's method is to select an enormous number
of quotations from Rahel's writing, analyze them, and provide them
with their cultural, historical, and literary contexts as she understood
them from her (historical) vantage point. With formidable sophistica-
tion, Arendt weaves together the Jewish Question and German Romanticism against a background of the breakdown of the aristocracy and
waning Enlightenment and the simultaneous rise of the bourgeoisie and
anti-Semitism. Hers was an unusually erudite knowledge of Rahel's moment in history—already a great deal more than Rahel knew or could
ever have known.

More contradictory yet, in the chapter "Night and Day" (which
appears in the middle of the book and, curiously, is the only one left
undated), Arendt analyzes several of Rahel's dreams. Her analysis is not
done in the Freudian manner, but she develops a theory of the separation
in Rahel's life of the days and nights that is lightly, but distinctly,
flavored by a simplified version of Freud's notion of manifest and latent
content. Arendt theorizes that what Rahel suppressed (and eventually
repressed) during the day—namely, the loss of two men with whom she
had been in love—appeared to her repeatedly in her dreams, with the
result that

> everything . . . took on the color of ambiguity, of a barely con-
> scious, by no means desired ambiguity. Recurrent dreams, nights
> which had specific testimony to give, would certainly not conjure
> up a life continuity of their own. But when a dream landscape has
> become known and familiar, it is easy to let oneself be drawn into
> it, as though there existed alongside the clear reality of the day a
> second land in which one would establish oneself comfortably.
> Once consciousness is clouded, once it is no longer certain that only
> one single world accompanies and surrounds us from birth to death,

ambiguity enters of its own accord, like twilight in the interval of day and night. The disgrace which no man and no God can remove, is by day an obsessional idea. Moving on, assimilation, learning history, are at night a comically hopeless game. When such a gulf yawns, only ambiguity points a permanent way out, by taking neither extreme seriously and engendering, in the twilight in which both extremes are mixed, resignation and new strength. (*RV* 143)

Arendt, though trying not to resort to unconscious mechanisms for explanations, gives a fairly accurate description in her rather overly literal terms of how the unconscious might function. From this awareness of being able to live in two "lands" at once, Arendt arrived at her notion of ambiguity, a state of mind to which she herself was given. "In her own time," writes her biographer, Elizabeth Young-Bruehl, "this was also Hannah Arendt's answer: neither assimilation nor Zionism, but ambiguity" (89).

Arendt does not acknowledge this state of mind in her preface (nor is any other information about her private or inner life released to the public until after her death and the publication of Young-Bruehl's book). Rather Arendt uses the preface to establish a place for herself outside or in the margins of the text—a place whose existence has been questioned since Derrida—from which she can speak of her intentions, the possible shortcomings and idiosyncracies of the text. In doing so she signals them and calls attention to the possibility that the text may be beyond her disclaimers and rationalizations, that it is out of her hands. The text exceeds her grasp, even as she attempts to take hold of it by means of the preface, in which she protests that she is allowing the text to speak for itself. Prefaces, as Derrida teaches, are never what they announce themselves to be: they are neither prior to the text nor outside it, as if behind an impermeable membrane. The preface/text binary is, he has shown, open at both ends. In his words, "the preface is a fiction . . . in the service of meaning" (*Dissemination* 35–36). It is a pretext for the reader that celebrates the stopping of the writing, its pastness, the moment that—in the conspicuous parentheses of such thought—is after(words) that becomes (a) post(face). It recalls the writer's desire for the text and his or her reading of it blinded by that desire.

Arendt's preface is inserted between the text and its epigraph, as if to bestow its mastery over both. The epigraph, however, tells us plainly what the text has in store:

We tell you, tapping on our brows,
   The story as it should be,—
As if the story of a house
   Were told or ever could be;
We'll have no kindly veil between
   Her visions and those we have seen,—
As if we guessed what hers have been
   Or what they are or would be. (my emphasis)

Despite whatever ironies may be embedded in this verse, the emphasized lines indicate that Arendt will be as much in her book as Rahel, its subject. I have given here only one of the two stanzas that comprise the untitled epigraph—the other tells of enduring "what God has given." These are the last two stanzas of a six-stanza poem by Edward Arlington Robinson called "Eros Tyrannos," a title that for Arendt at least could not fail to elicit the pathos and ambiguities of self-knowledge evoked by *Oedipus Tyrannos*. Omitted (suppressed?) are not only the title of the poem but those stanzas dealing directly with the poem's subject: passionate, tyrannical love. The omissions are significant as a possible form of self-censorship, because the text concerns itself with the power love has not only over Rahel but over Arendt. She wrote the biography some years after a secret, passionate love affair she, at eighteen, had with her professor Martin Heidegger, seventeen years her senior.

Before writing *Rahel Varnhagen*, Arendt, a closet poet for much of her early life, had tried to write Heidegger out of her system in a long Romantic poem called "The Shadows" ("Die Schatten"), but to no avail. As Young-Bruehl writes, "Hannah Arendt had to tell someone else's story, had to write *Rahel Varnhagen: The Life of a Jewess*, before she freed herself from Martin Heidegger's spell" (50). In this biography, Arendt managed not only to think through the Jewish Question, and Rahel's (and her own) relation to the world as Jews, but to put into perspective, through her work on Rahel, her strong tendency toward introspection and melancholy intensified by the unsatisfactory ending of a deep passion, a first love, that had left her alone and alienated. By writing *Rahel Varnhagen*, Arendt wrote herself into the world: this bildungsroman of Rahel is Arendt's as well.

The state of ambiguity Arendt ascribed to Rahel was the very means by which she negotiated her own inner and outer worlds and her relation to the difficult political issues she faced. An important aspect of Arendt's ambiguity, however, was her ability to suspend it when necessary. When attacked as a Jew, she responded as one, and so, although she was not a Zionist, she worked at times for Zionist causes. When the Nazi SS were rounding up Communists, she hid them in her apartment, although she herself was not a Communist. When the issues at hand required action, she acted. Commitments to ideologies, however, were another matter for Arendt. She did not want to become part of any establishment, or even part of any group outside an establishment. Not only was she a conscious pariah (an idea she derived from the work of Bernard Lazare [see p. 119]), but like her friend Walter Benjamin, Arendt "was a pariah within the *Pariahvolk*" (Young-Bruehl 168).

Arendt's ambiguity may have been responsible for her being a protofeminist, even though she did not address the "Woman Problem" in the biography because, as she wrote in the preface,

> the Woman Problem, that is the discrepancy between what men expected of women "in general" and what women could give or wanted in their turn, was already established by the condition of the era and represented a gap that virtually could not be closed. (*RV* xviii)

Nonetheless, the "Woman Problem" is addressed in the text, even articulated. It is a subtext of the book announced by its subtitle, *The Life of a Jewess,* or its contemporary version, *The Life of a Jewish Woman.* Although the word *Jewess* has become two words in the revised title, the idea of Jew and woman cannot be separated in the title or in the book. Rahel, the woman, is powerfully portrayed as Bedford points out in her review: "One is made to feel the subject, the waiting, distraught woman; one is made aware almost physically, of her intense femininity, her frustration" ("Emancipation and Destiny" 23). From the outset, Arendt presents the conditions that have to do with Rahel not just as a Jew, but, as the opening chapter says, as a "Jewess and Schlemiel." The conditions that contrive to make her a schlemiel, who is, as Arendt explains, "a hapless human being . . . who has anticipated nothing" (*RV* 6), are as much concerned with her being a woman as a Jew.

Although born into a rich family, Rahel had no formal education, and after her father died, she was left with no money of her own. Her resources seriously diminished, Rahel had very little with which to save herself from remaining a Jew. "Only failures and 'schlemihls,' it would seem, were left behind within the German-Jewish society," writes Arendt (*RV* 6). Moreover, Rahel had none of the innate gifts many women are able to call on to help them move through society. According to Arendt, "Beauty in a woman can mean power and Jewish girls were frequently not married for their dowries alone. With Rahel, however, nature went to no great trouble" (*RV* 6). As Rahel puts it,

> "I have no grace. . . . In addition to not being pretty, I have also no inner grace. . . . I am unprepossessing rather than ugly. . . . Some people have not a single praiseworthy proportion, and yet they make a pleasing impression. . . . With me it is just the opposite." (*RV* 6)

Arendt knew very well what such a shortcoming could mean:

> In a woman beauty creates a perspective from which she can judge and choose. Neither intelligence nor experience can make up for the lack of that natural perspective. Not rich, not cultivated and not beautiful—that meant that she [Rahel] *was entirely without weapons* with which to begin the great struggle for recognition in society, for social existence, for a morsel of happiness, for security and an established position in the bourgeois world. (*RV* 6; my emphasis)

Being a woman, neither rich nor beautiful, and Jewish confirmed Rahel's position as that of a schlemiel—one that she resisted and continued to fight against and lose until she was forty-three, when she married Karl August Varnhagen (who was twenty-nine) and became Frau Fredericke Varnhagen von Ense. Only after this marriage (preceeded by a broken engagement to a count and an intense, but short-lived, love affair with a Spanish diplomat) did she realize what it meant to be a woman parvenu: "Now I have to behave toward people as if I were nothing more than *my husband;* in the past I was *nothing,* and that was a great deal" (*RV* 210; emphasis in original). Arendt treats the implications of Rahel's womanhood as well as her Jewishness. For Arendt, they are inseparable as a way to understand Rahel. As a way to see the mechanisms of exclusion, analyzing the two together is invaluable.

That Arendt discusses so clearly and carefully the relation of a woman's beauty to her positions in the (man's) world and omits the details of the situation in which Rahel was able to surround herself with a coterie of illustrious intellectuals and set up a salon in the attic apartment of her parents' home when she was only in her very early twenties demonstrates her primary interest in the generalities that Rahel's writings produce. Although Arendt's cry is for experience—no idea without experience—her enterprise is not to chronicle its data but to put that experience into perspective, into a framework by which it is transmuted into a generalization that does not falsify but finds out experience, discovers it, (re)invents it, and sees it freshly illuminated. Her desire is to move the experience of the private, of the individual, into a public realm of discourse where the experience of women as well as men becomes reconstituted into a historical and political context (see chapter 1, pp. 12–15, for my explanation of Arendt's public and private realms). She does not see the two realms as mutually exclusive, with the private realm the domain of women and the public of men (albeit that is how it has been historically). She sees that women, despite their biology and social roles can, indeed must, be part of the political realm as well. I strongly object to Mary O'Brien's claim that Arendt believes in a "second [and higher] nature for men that becomes visible in the public realm" (100–101). Nowhere in her work does Arendt indicate or suggest that women are of a different nature from men that keeps them out of the public realm. They are outside it for cultural and historical, not natural, reasons. It seems to me that Arendt's project (prototypical of today's feminist goals) is to put Rahel's life of ideas into the mainstream of German-Jewish history in particular and into the diaspora in general.

The experience of Jewish women, as Arendt sees it in *Rahel Varnhagen,* is not just the stuff of private confession, inconsequential and trivial, it is part of an outside, a foreign territory, that exists at the borders of an inside. The demarcation between the two is the boundary—the law—literally a wall that encloses the political space: "The word *polis* originally connoted something like a 'ring-wall'" (*HC* 64). The composition of the outside changes from time to time as does the inside.

Actors and Jews, among them women, accepted by the nobility, were excluded from society by the new and growing middle class of Rahel's time. The salons of the day, bringing together people of all classes and some who did not fit anywhere, were run often by Jewish women—Henrietta Herz; Dorothea Mendelssohn Schlegel; the Meier sisters, Marianne, married to a prince, and Sarah to a baron; and the Itzig sisters, Frau von Eskeles and Frau von Arnstein—"who were actually the agents of social assimilation" (*RV* 33). Once the age of benevolence to Jews under Frederick II was over, other groups (which included some of the younger Romantics) were formed based on exclusivity—secret societies—that banned the admittance of women, Frenchmen, philistines, and Jews (the last three representative of the Enlightenment). As Arendt writes, "the exclusion of women must be understood as a direct protest against the Jewish salons of the day" (*RV* 124).

Wherever there are outsiders, there are women. Arendt did not see them as separable from the general plight of the exclusion of Jews or anyone else. As for the inequality women suffered at the hands of the men within their own group, she thought that should be addressed as political gains are achieved by the whole group. Young-Bruehl writes of Arendt: "What she wanted for women and from women was attention paid to questions about political and legal discrimination, attention broad enough to relate women's political and legal problems to those of all groups denied equality" (273).

The divisions of life into two departments, public and private, leads to assumptions that they are binary oppositions and mutually exclusive. I suggest they are not; at least, they need not be treated as such. People move back and forth between them. Both/and is at play here—a strong reflection of Arendt's ambiguity—not either/or. No one, not even a woman, can live a full or free life without access to the public realm. I see a strong correspondence in the movement between the two realms with the psychic movement between the Lacanian agencies of the imaginary (a kind of preverbal register of the mother, of the specular, the image, the part-object, of aggressivity and narcissism) and the symbolic (the register of the father, of language and culture). There can be no entry into the symbolic without passing through the imaginary, nor can a person take his or her place in society as a functional individual without access to the symbolic. A person cannot reside exclusively in one or the other, but each individual exists in an oscillation between the two in the constitution of his or her subjectivity (in language).

So, in Arendt's notion of the public and private realms, the social existence of an individual is constituted by his or her movement between the two realms. Just as not having "a private place of one's own is to be no longer human" (*HC* 64), there is also no possibility of a functioning citizen outside the public realm. When, depending on the political exigencies of a particular moment, the public realm denies entry to some, is weak, or even disappears, the constitution of the individual citizen, who may act in concert with other citizens as a duly established body, is prevented, and freedom is abrogated. The result is increased isolation, until "self and world, capacity for thought and experience are lost at the same time" (*OT* 3:175).

Rahel's ambition, her desire for a place in the world, kept her from totally surrendering to isolation, to worldlessness. After a run of bad luck (it seemed to her that chance, fate, were her constant companions in life), she gave up trying to find someone who would raise her to the top. Instead she found a man, who although not a Jew was nonetheless a parvenu (*RV* 182), with whom she could rise. She inoculated Karl Varnhagen with her ambition and energy, but he also put Rahel forward. He collated everything she had ever written to him about Goethe, provided some of his own responses, and had all of it published in a small volume (*RV* 188). It was Goethe's first impression that the initials given as Varnhagen's in the correspondence were the woman's, and those of Rahel's the man's. But as noted earlier, we cannot always (ever?) tell the sex of the writer from the writing. He praised Rahel lavishly: "The woman does not actually judge; she *has* the subject, and insofar as she does not possess it, it does not concern her" (*RV* 188). Given this accolade, the reader can understand Goethe's initial mistaking of identities. Possessing the subject was in those days considered a masculine endeavor—and still is considered a phallocentric activity, even in the hands of women.

Rahel did not, however, "exploit this triumph" (*RV* 189). Goethe was the one person she never even attempted to know socially, because he was so consequential in her development as an intellectual woman—as a reader and a thinker. Through his books, she found her language, her understanding of history. She wrote of him:

> His riches gave me company; he has eternally been my sole and surest friend . . . eternally my guarantor that I do not merely live fearfully among fleeting ghosts, my superior master, my compassionate friend; of him I knew what hells he had looked into. . . . In short, I grew up with him, and after a thousand separations I always found him again; he never failed me. (*RV* 113–14)

Arendt commented:

> It was the great good fortune of Rahel's that she found the one person she had trusted. It was her great opportunity to confide in

history, in language. . . . Only in the wholly liberated purity of the poetic, in which all words are, as it were, spoken for the first time, can language become her friend, one to whom she is willing to entrust herself and her unprecedented life. Goethe provided her with the language to speak. . . . *Again and again his words freed her from the mute spell of mere happening.* And her ability to speak provided her with an asylum in the world, taught her how to trust what she had heard. She had Goethe to thank for being able to speak. (*RV* 115; my emphasis)

Rahel and Arendt enjoyed language and looked to men as exemplars. Arendt looked to Heidegger, who taught her "passionate thinking" and *Existenz* philosophy; to Jaspers, with whom she wrote her dissertation, and who remained her fatherly interlocutor (her father died when she was seven) until his death in 1969; and to Walter Benjamin (in her flight from the Nazis, she carried with her the manuscripts for the text that became *Illuminations*), whose work reinforced her love of language and quotation, her sense of the complexity of history, and even her ambiguity. But neither of them turned away from women or denied their own femininity (both had very close women friends).

The spatial relation of *between* is central to many of Arendt's formu-

Although Goethe had at first mistaken her for a man by her writing, Rahel reacted to him, when he paid her a brief visit, in a most feminine way, as Arendt understood it and admired it. On learning that he was in Frankfort, Rahel sent him a short note, to which he responded by appearing at her door without prior warning. When word of her visitor was given her, she was not "dressed." She had him admitted and donned a plain black skirt in which she presented herself to him "in order not to make him wait a moment longer." Of this, Arendt writes approvingly, "A greater display of modesty, than not to dress in order not to make the man 'wait a moment longer' would scarcely be offered by a woman to a man" (*RV* 189). When Goethe left, Rahel performed a wonderfully feminine act that Arendt does not fail to include: "After he was gone, I dressed up very fine, as though I wanted to make up for it all. A lovely white dress with high collar, a lace coif and veil, the Moscow shawl" (*RV* 189). Neither Rahel nor Arendt was bound by the received opinion of what women were supposed to be like. They constituted their femininity on their own terms—somewhere between what was expected of them and what they desired for themselves.

The spatial relation of *between* is central to many of Arendt's formulations. In a variation of Heidegger's ontological notion that each of us "lingers awhile . . . , com[ing] to presence in the 'between' of a twofold absence" (*Early Greek Thinking* 48), Arendt sees us as living *between* natality—a term she developed to indicate the importance of each new birth as a new beginning, as a possibility of beginning something new, of acting (*HC* 9)—and mortality (also mentioned in chapter 1, p. 14). In addition to moving between the public and the private realms, an individual moves between thinking (*la vita contemplativa*) and acting (*la vita activa*), and his or her thoughts exist in a now that is carved out "between past and future"—the title Arendt gave a collection of her essays. The idea in the title comes from her reading of one of Kafka's aphorisms (from a series, "He") which Arendt calls an "experience in thinking" (*BPF* 14). As Arendt puts it, the parable he uses is

> a real παραβολαί [*parábolai*] thrown alongside and around the incident like rays of light which, however, do not illuminate its outward appearance but possess the power of X-rays to lay bare its inner structure that . . . [here] consists of the hidden processes of the mind. (*BPF* 7)

Kafka's writes:

> He has two antagonists: the first presses him from behind, for the origin. The second blocks the road ahead. He gives battle to both. To be sure, the first supports him in his fight with the second, for he wants to push him forward, and in the same way the second supports him in his fight with the first, since he drives him back. But it is only theoretically so. For it is not only the two antagonists who are there, but he himself as well, and who really knows his intentions? His dream, though, is that sometime in an unguarded moment—and this would require a night darker than any night has ever been yet—he will jump out of the fighting line and be promoted, on account of his experience in fighting, to the position of umpire over his antagonists in their fight with each other. (*BPF* 7)

In Arendt's agile and powerful reading is the insertion of an individual ("he") between two antagonistic forces, past and future, to which, to stand "his" ground, "he" must give battle (throughout her explication, Arendt uses quotation marks to indicate Kafka's protagonist, although Kafka does not). The past pushes "him" ahead in "his" fight with the future, which, in turn, drives "him" back to face the past. "He" lives in the interval between past and future, and from "his" standpoint, time is not a continuum; it is broken in the middle where "he" stands. Arendt observes, "Only because man is inserted into time and only to the extent that he stands his ground does the flow of indifferent time break up into tenses" (*BPF* 12). "He" becomes a diagonal between the antagonists (whose forces have been deflected by "him" from their original directions to meet at an angle), which, as Arendt interprets, is

> the path paved by thinking, this small track of non-time which the activity of thought beats within the time-space of mortal men and into which the trains of thought, of remembrance and anticipation, save whatever they touch from the ruin of historical and biographical time. This small non-time-space in the very heart of time, unlike the world and culture into which we are born, can only be indicated, but cannot be inherited and handed down from the past; each new generation, indeed every human being as he inserts himself between an infinite past and an infinite future, must discover and ploddingly pave it anew. (*BPF* 13)

This path of thinking is paved with difference, with discreteness, and with the distinctions that are the individual stories gleaned from experience that keep us from being swept up by the utopian promises of ideologies, by received opinion, or by the rule of nobody, Arendt's phrase for bureaucracy in which nobody is responsible for anything, orders are followed, and the system grinds on and over everybody.

Arendt uses the notion of *between* not only to indicate a mental locus but to suggest a distance that is a range of discrete behaviors and conventions (social and legal) that can be analyzed. She has a section in *Antisemitism* called "Between Vice and Crime," in which she discusses briefly, in her own words:

> the transformation of the "crime" of Judaism into the fashionable "vice" of Jewishness [which] was dangerous in the extreme. Jews had been able to escape Judaism into conversion. From Jewishness there was no escape [a realization that Rahel came upon in her later years]. A crime, moreover, is met with punishment; a vice can only be exterminated. (*OT* 1:87)

In this section, Arendt discusses the connection that was made in the late nineteenth century between the "vice" of Jewishness and another so-called vice, homosexuality (the brutal treatment of homosexuals by the Nazis is well known), the combination of these two strains of difference in the person of Marcel Proust, and his incomparable depiction of both in French society (during the time of the Dreyfus Affair) in his *A la recherche du temps perdu,* an aspect of which I referred to in my reading of Duras (p. 94).

Antisemitism also contains a section called "Between Pariah and Parvenu," the same title as the penultimate chapter of *Rahel Varnhagen* (with the addition of the dates 1815–1819 in parenthesis to indicate the years of Rahel's life under discussion). Written in Paris in 1938, five years after Arendt had finished the others, this chapter and the next ("One Does Not Escape Jewishness [1820–1833]") contain a feeling of conclusion and climax. Its tone gives the feeling of summary, of summation, and of the essayistic. It is a tone of the liveliest and most passionate kind—the beginnings of the Arendt style (her storytelling) with which her readers from the fifties on became familiar. These chapters bring Rahel's "life" to a close as her understanding of the world and her place in it opens. At the same time, crossing Rahel's story is Arendt's history of the Jews in Germany, in which any hope of legal status (the gaining of rights that would put them on the inside) comes to a close, and in which the "crime" of Judaism is on its way to becoming the "vice" of Jewishness that by 1938 opens the door to extermination. It was the beginning of the end. These openings and closings, beginnings and endings suggest the superimposition of the microcosmic and macrocosmic standpoints— the development of an individual life as seen against the forces of history—that produces such intersections, the configurations of which can be perceived as resulting in a chiasmic relation, the crossing of strains (story and history) marked as a space of writing—the scene of Arendt's writing.

Each story she tells has as its kernel an experience that is her ground, her place from which she does the "drilling" of the depths in which the past is sunk to wrest from it and gather about herself "thought fragments" that have suffered a "sea-change." She wrote about these ideas in her introduction to Benjamin's *Illuminations,* describing his "gift of thinking poetically," especially in regard to his use of quotation (*MDT* 203–5). In a world that has to look at its past without the aid of tradition, quoting from the past takes place with the conviction that the "process of decay is at the same time a process of crystallization" (*MDT* 206), and that one can tear out these fragments (crystallizations) from their old moorings and see perhaps some "rich and strange" promise they may hold for us. As Benjamin wrote, "History is the subject of a structure whose site is not homogeneous, empty time, but time filled by the presence of the now [*jetztzeit*]" (*Illuminations* 261).

The method of quotation and commentary, that Arendt uses in *Rahel Varnhagen* and her other works is her way of both destroying and preserving the past. It is the means by which she (like Kafka's "he") grabs hold of now in a struggle with those sempiternal antagonists, past and future. That struggle is the making of stories, her thought trains, that articulate (with) history so that the future is approached looking backward—a kind of demonstration of the future anterior (see chapter 2, pp. 54–55), a tense that inheres in the notion of the postmodern, and of Benjamin's view of progress as a storm blowing from Paradise, irresistibly propelling the individual into the future, to which his or her back is turned (*Illuminations* 258).

In this limited sense, Arendt is a protopostmodernist—definitely between past and future. Significantly, she thought *Between Past and Future* was the best of her books: "She believed in its form" (Young-Bruehl 473). As suggested by its subtitle, *Eight Exercises in Political Thought,* it was not systematic. It was experimental. As Arendt wrote in her preface to that book,

> Since these exercises move between past and future, they contain criticism as well as experiment, but the experiments do not attempt to design some sort of utopian future, and the critique of the past, of traditional concepts, does not intend to "debunk." (*MDT* 14)

She did not see a sharp division between the critical and experimental parts of the book, because there is an element of experiment in the critical interpretation of the past (*MDT* 15) that seeks to discover, find, "to distill anew . . . [the] original spirit [of traditional concepts] which has so sadly evaporated from the very key words of the political language" (*MDT* 15). She saw the essay as the "literary form [that] has the closest affinity to the exercises I have in mind" (*MDT* 15). This inclination toward experimentation can be seen in *Rahel Varnhagen,* an experimental biography ("this book was conceived and written from an angle unusual in biographical literature" [*RV* xv]). It is what I would call a biographical essay.

The close connection between experiment and essay in the senses of trying, testing, and writing (see chapter 1, p. 24) and the notion that what is tested, tried (trials as both experiments and legal proceedings are embedded here and germane), and written is experience seem evident to Arendt. Hence both a cognate and an actual relation exists among the three words *experience, experiment,* and *essay.* Arendt's experiments are a trying out, a way of discovering, of finding meaning. Finding is closely related to invention. Writing as an invention of experience not only suggests the creation of fantasies (something that never existed before) but points to a certain experimentation with the telling of experience that brings understanding and reconciliation. Arendt's biography (with its autobiographical currents) is as much a meditation on Rahel's life as it is the recounting of it (I am reminded here of Margaret Drabble's later work). Arendt wrote of Rahel, a Jewish woman—and thus wrote of Jews and women—discovering, among other things, the inner and outer mise-en-scène of the well-traveled avenue between pariah and parvenu.

Though Rahel would not use Goethe himself for social climbing, in the nineteenth century, literary distinction became a means by which a writer established himself or herself in society, and the Varnhagens threw themselves into literature. Their salon formed the center of the Goethe cult in Berlin—quite a different affair from the one Rahel had had in her garret some thirty years earlier. As Arendt put it, "The extent to which the Berlin cult concealed parvenu manners was suspected by no one, save young Heine" (*RV* 204). The Jewish-German poet Heinrich Heine and Rahel were great friends. "Only galley slaves know one another" was Rahel's phrase of recognition for the two Jewish men she met in society with whom she became close friends: David Veit, a medical student, in her youth, and Heine in her mature years (*RV* 25, 227). In one of his letters to her, the assimilated Heine wrote that he promised to be "enthusiastic for the cause of Jews and their attainment of equality before the law. In bad times, which are inevitable, the Germanic rabble will hear my voice ring resoundingly in German beer halls and palaces." This "affirmation of Jewishness," remarks Arendt, was "the first and last resolute affirmation which was to be heard from an assimilated Jew for a long time" (*RV* 227).

In *Rahel Varnhagen,* Arendt began to develop her notion of the Jews as a "pariah people"—a term of Max Weber's (Arendt, "JP" 69). In her 1944 essay "The Jew as Pariah," she showed how Jewish artists and writers (doubly exiled often as Jews *and* artists) have been able to evolve out of their personal experience the concept of the pariah as a human type that, having endured from the eighteenth century to the twentieth, has become traditional ("JP" 68). Out of the variety of forms this type can assume, Arendt presents four, each of which expresses an alternative portrayal of the Jewish people by a different artist.

First, Arendt mentions "Heinrich Heine: The Schlemihl and Lord of Dreams." Heine portrays the Jewish people as filled with a joie de vivre and love for the "divine realities of nature"—the sun, music, trees, and children—outside the pale of the social and political world, with himself as their poet-king ("JP" 71). Second, she mentions the Jewish-French writer and journalist "Bernard Lazare: The Conscious Pariah." Lazare felt it was necessary to rouse the Jewish pariah to fight against the Jewish parvenu. He saw the Jew as doubly enslaved by "'the wealthy of my people, who exploit me and sell me . . . [and] by the rich and the poor of other peoples who oppress and torture me in the name of my rich'" ("JP" 77). He saw that the emancipated Jew must become a rebel against it, or he will be complicit in maintaining the pariah-parvenu circuit ("JP" 76–79).

Third, Arendt mentions the English film artist "Charlie Chaplin: The Suspect" (of whom Arendt notes that he had declared himself to be of Irish descent, but, she insists, "even if not himself a Jew, he has epitomized in an artistic form a character born of the Jewish pariah mentality" ["JP" 69]). Standing outside the pale, always suspected by a world that he is basically at odds with, was the little tramp, the Chaplin pariah who could not fail to arouse the sympathy of the common people and become an idol of the masses ("JP" 79). Fourth, she mentions the Jewish-Czech writer (who wrote in German) "Franz Kafka: The Man of Goodwill." Kafka, in his *Description of a Fight,* shows that the use of the contemplative faculty as an instrument of self-preservation character-izes his conception of the pariah. Also, K in Kafka's *The Castle* exhausts himself in his struggle to determine his existence by simply exercising, as a man of goodwill, his normal human rights ("JP" 83, 85–87).

Heine, a conscious pariah, "the only German Jew who could truth-fully describe himself as both a German and a Jew" ("JP" 74), made no concessions to either parvenu Jews or German society about the gran-deur and the misery, the good and the not-so-good, of the ordinary, garden variety Jew from whom Jewishness came—exactly what those allowed into favor, the assimilated exceptions, wanted to extirpate from their lives. By virtue of his artistry, he did what previously had been zealously avoided. By introducing Yiddish expressions into the German language (the word, *schlemiel,* for example, which has also entered the English language according to *The American Heritage Dictionary*) and by his subject matter, he effected a blending of the cultures ("JP" 74).

Heine became Rahel's spiritual heir. She could die a bit more peacefully trusting that he would be able to put to good use her "history of bankruptcy [her parvenuism] and her rebellious spirit" (*RV* 228). "I am a rebel after all!" (*RV* 224), she realized just as she achieved her parvenu ends. Arendt closes the biography with a lovely passage—Rahel's very literary last will and testament—directed to Heine.

> No philanthropic list, no cheers, no condescension, no mixed society, no new hymn book, no bourgeois star, nothing, nothing could ever placate me. . . . *You* will say this gloriously, elegaically, fantastically, incisively, extremely jestingly, always musically, provokingly, often charmingly; you will say it all very soon. But as you do, the text from my old offended heart will still have to remain yours. (*RV* 228)

Perversely, Rahel's rebellious spirit had taken hold once she "arrived." Once she had become, in Baden, a Prussian citizen and was simply the wife of the Prussian chargé d'affaires (*RV* 202), she found she could not pay the price of remaining a parvenu. Her past had been far too rich with experience. She had already suffered too much indignity to deny that she was an alien, that hers was an alien and ancient past. As she wrote—a quotation with which Arendt opens the biography—

> What a history!—A fugitive from Egypt and Palestine, here I am and find help, love, fostering in you people. With real rapture I think of these origins of mine and this whole nexus of destiny, through which the oldest of the human race stand side by side with the latest developments. The greatest distances in time and space are bridged. The thing which all my life seemed to me the greatest shame, which was the misery and misfortune of my life—having been born a Jewess—this I would on no account now wished to have missed. (*RV* 3)

The distance between the opening and the closing of the book is filled with Rahel's errantry/errancy and Arendt's trailblazing as both move through pages of writing. It took Rahel a lifetime to find her place in the world, and once she found it, she realized that although she had been allowed to slip through the legal crack to the inside, that place was still on the outside. The distance between the pariah and the parvenu is both infinite and infinitesimal. "And so," notes Arendt, "at the end of her life she [Rahel] wrote whole paragraphs in her letters to her brother in Hebrew characters, just as she had done in her girlhood" (*RV* 227).

Rahel could abandon neither her past pariah status nor her present parvenu position, no matter how little, in reality, the latter afforded her. So, as if to acknowledge that past, while still in Baden enjoying her new "civility," Rahel asked Varnhagen who was attending peace conferences in Paris to locate "the most compromised of her friends of her youth, Pauline Wiesel," the former mistress of Prince Louis Ferdinand, both of whom had attended Rahel's garret salon. Wiesel was the only woman Rahel ever thought of as her equal. As she wrote to a friend in 1816, Pauline is

one who knows nature and the world as we do . . . , who is surprised at nothing unusual and who is eternally preoccupied with the mysteriousness of the usual; who has loved and been loved like us; who can no longer endure loneliness and cannot be without it . . . , who has had the absurdly wonderful fortune to encounter one other person who sees things the same way and who is alike, though her talents are so different—which only makes it all the more amusing.

Wiesel had been much loved in her youth because of "her great beauty and amazing, dismaying naturalness" (*RV* 206).

Arendt, too, in yet another remarkable parallel with Rahel, had a close woman friend also endowed with an overwhelming naturalness that was endlessly fascinating to Arendt. She was flattered that her friend, Hilde Frankel saw in her a kindred soul (Young-Bruehl 242). Frankel was a longtime mistress of Paul Tillich, the Christian theologian, whom Arendt also knew. The two women met in Frankfort around 1930, rediscovered each other in New York during the war, and formed a deep bond of friendship that lasted until Frankel's death in 1950. She was different from Arendt's other friends—she was not a writer or an intellectual. She had "lived." She was worldly wise, with a great warmth and generosity of spirit. As Arendt described her, she was "gifted with erotic genius"; she "understood, so to speak, everything" (Young-

Bruehl 240, 243). In a letter to Frankel that has some affinity with Rahel's remarks about Wiesel, Arendt openly expressed her gratitude,

> not only for the kind of relaxation which comes from an intimacy like none I have ever known with a woman, but also for the unforgettable good fortune of our nearness, a good fortune which is all the greater because you are not an "intellectual" (a hateful word) and therefore are a confirmation of my very self and of my true beliefs. (Young-Bruehl 240)

Frankel, in turn, admired and trusted Arendt, "the only person in my life to whom I speak fully and completely," not because of her intellectual gifts, but for simply being in Frankel's words "what you especially are—a woman'" (Young-Bruehl 243).

All her so-called masculine endeavors, her intellectual proclivities, did not obscure Arendt's womanhood or the recognition of it by both men (among whom she had many passionate admirers) and women. She had a gift for friendship and had several abiding ones with women besides Frankel. Her girlhood friend Anne Mendelssohn (a descendant of Moses and Felix) Weil, who studied philosophy with Ernst Cassirer, who had actually introduced Arendt to Rahel Varnhagen, and to whom Arendt dedicated the biography, remained her *beste freundin* even through years of estrangement caused by the vicissitudes of exile (Weil had settled in Paris), until Arendt's death fifty-five years later.

In the early 1950s, Arendt became very close friends with the essayist and novelist Mary McCarthy, whose work she admired, and in whom she found that worldly innocence she attributed to conscious pariahs, an attribute she herself had in no small measure. As she put it to McCarthy, "we two think so much alike" (Young-Bruehl 197). The dedication to *Crises of the Republic* (three long essays: "Lying in Politics: Reflection on the Pentagon Papers," "Civil Disobedience," and "On Violence") read, "for Mary McCarthy in friendship." After Arendt died, McCarthy became her literary executor and editor of the posthumous *Life of the Mind,* Arendt's return to ("pure") philosophy on the issues of thinking, willing, and judging—the last left unfinished. The combination of innocence and wide experience, so attractive to Arendt, is a rebel quality as she saw it, fed by an innocence preserved. It is a little space (a patch of schlemieldom) that does not become violated by (too much) experience and that guards against corrosive cynicism or crippling ineffectualism. Arendt recognized in Frankel, too, that special difference found in outsiders, just as one hundred years before, Rahel had seen it in Pauline Wiesel.

Rahel, nominally on the inside, aligning herself with Wiesel, unmistakably on the outside, writes:

> We have been created to live the truth in this world. . . . We are *alongside* human society. For us no place, no office, no empty title exists! *All* lies have someplace; eternal truth, proper living and feeling . . . has no place! And thus we are excluded from society. You because you offended it. . . . I because I cannot sin and lie along with it. (*RV* 202)

Although their friendship lasted until Rahel died, it was not uncomplicated. Wiesel was difficult and disruptive. She even turned her seductive arts toward Varnhagen himself ("to taste Rahel's husband—like iced punch"), which upset him more than it did Rahel, who tried vainly to explain that "this attempt at seduction was proof of the interest [Wiesel's] in Rahel's own fate" (*RV* 207).

After Rahel's death, Varnhagen sought his revenge (while indulging in unbridled parvenuism) by paying Wiesel, who had become old, impoverished, and ill, a ducat for each of Rahel's letters and erasing her, literally, from Rahel's life. He published Rahel's letters and diary entries in a three-volume *Buch des Andenkens, 1834*, in which he made wholesale corrections, interpolations, and mutilations, expunged portions, and coded personal names so that readers were led astray (*RV* xiv-xv). The significant fact of this bowdlerization (which is well documented) is, Arendt declares,

> that almost all his omissions and misleading codings of names were intended to make Rahel's associations and circle of friends appear less Jewish and more aristocratic, and to show Rahel herself in a more conventional light, and more in keeping with the taste of the time. (*RV* xv)

He left the entire correspondence between Wiesel and Rahel unpublished (with the exception of a few extracts that he published without using Wiesel's name or, inexplicably, under the initials Fr. v. V. (*RV* xv). Although, historically, such unauthorized revision of another's writing has not necessarily been a matter of gender, that Rahel was his wife—and therefore, to use her words, "nothing more than her husband"—and a Jew gave Varnhagen license to violate her body of writing to eradicate her difference and secure her position, even in death, on the inside, to reduce her (as much as he could) to the same and elevate himself.

All her life, Rahel had admired this woman whom her husband found so reprehensible. She believed that between her and her friend was only one difference: "You *live* everything because you have the courage and have had the luck; I *think* most things because I have had no luck and have acquired no courage." In Arendt's eyes:

> Pauline exercised *utter freedom* in placing herself outside the pale of respectable society because her temperamental and untamable nature would submit to no conventions. Her courage was her naturalness, which was supported and strengthened by all those who fled society to her, and made a free life possible for her. (*RV* 208; my emphasis).

Once she recognized how impoverished the position she had achieved (at great cost) was, Rahel, too, courageously exercised "utter freedom," by embracing a woman pariah as her friend.

Freedom, a central concept of Arendt's, is the condition of thinking and acting, of finding a place, a way to be in relation to the world. Although coeval with the creation of human beings (*HC* 177) and reestablished with each new beginning or birth, such freedom, for women especially, has been foreclosed on sociopolitical levels (and now on a number of theoretical ones formulated by women themselves), which has prevented them from behaving outside of accepted lines without paying the price—stigmatization or explusion (from the inside) or both. Overcoming these constraints is difficult enough, but even more difficult is the problem that faces women (and men) today: the assumption of the condition of freedom even though we know that we are each born into language, into a place in a culture that is determined by our relation to the dominant ideology and power structure of that culture.

Hence, for each one of us, exercising freedom always flies in the face of its impossibility. It becomes what might be called (perhaps even by Arendt) a necessary fiction. It becomes the tension between reality and desire. Women, in their desire for the equality that will end their silence and worldlessness, must think their freedom and act it without

being constrained by any totalizing narratives, even those in the service
of a feminism that in its ideological bent takes on another face of that old
master discourse humanism (read phallocracy), which women are trying
to deconstruct. But this must be done, paradoxically, without abandon-
ing the thrust of the feminist struggle to make women licit members of
the world. That struggle, with all its ambiguities and tensions, contradictions even, can be said to *be* freedom, making the word *freedom* not
just a description of a state but a condition of action. Freedom is not just
attained but practiced—always in public, in community with others. It
is not simply a goal but a field of existence that appears as one exercises
it. To borrow Plotinus's maxim (see p. 103), "We must seek the [free-
dom] we are seeking by means of the [freedom] we seek."

Arendt set up the basis for freedom in *The Human Condition,* in
which she discusses three human activities, labor, work, and action, that
correspond to the basic human conditions of life on earth: labor to life
itself (i.e., *natality, mortality,* and *earth*); work to *worldliness* (i.e., the
making of things not subjected to nature and its life cycles—an "artificial
world" distinctly different from all natural surroundings, meant to out-
last the individuals within that world); and action to *plurality* (i.e., "It is
men not Man, who live on earth and inhabit the world. While all aspects
of the human condition are somehow related to politics, this *plurality* is
specifically *the* condition of all political life" [*HC* 7]). The condition of
plurality appears in the public realm, the place where an in-between
functions as a means of bringing people together without removing the
distance (the ground) between them. Arendt explains that "we call this
reality [the in-between] the 'web' of human relationships, indicating by
this metaphor its somewhat intangible quality" (*HC* 183). In the realm
of human affairs, worldly interests lie between—"*inter-est*" (*HC* 182)—
people, separating *and* connecting them, creating relations that, as Arendt understood it from her reading of Montesquieu, is the Law:
"Law . . . is what relates, so that religious law is what relates man to
God and human law what relates men to their fellow men. . . . Without
human law space between men would be a desert, or rather there would
be no space at all" (*OR* 302).

So difficult, so deeply paradoxical about the struggle of feminists is
that they cannot do away with the law that both exiles them and keeps
them (*inter-est*) between people—that relates them to others and makes
them other—and that when they attempt to change the law they are
already in the phallocentric mode. They are no longer other but the

same. They have become men. By their own phallic thrust, feminists have put themselves into a theoretical impasse that can only be surmounted by a double vision and practice, a deconstructive practice that is not simply a subversion or a dismantling, both negativities, but a positive ambiguity that affirms a position, takes a stand, and sees the condition of its deconstruction at the same time.[2] It is important to keep in mind that deconstruction is not a body of information by which we refute arguments but "a practice *on* writing *in* writing" (Kamuf, "A Double Life" 96). The prototype for such an affirmative deconstruction, which is at once both conservative and radical, is the Arendtian ambiguity that I have been rehearsing. Furthermore, this ambiguity leads not necessarily to a simple bisexualism often seen as an erosion of difference or a blurring of distinctions but to a way of retaining distinctions and difference in all relations between the sexes. It is a refusal to give up distinctions by synthesizing them into seamless wholes that do not exist and into which nobody fits.

One distinction Arendt insisted on maintaining is the puristic separation between the private and the public realms. She consistently refused to give ground (up) to that area of human affairs called the social, a hybrid realm between the public and the private that has overtaken both. With the connection of economics since the eighteenth century (hitherto always in the realm of necessity, the private) to politics, nation states were run like vast households, giving rise to national bureaucracies—rule by nobody, as Arendt liked to say—at the expense of the public space. The space between people (that which distinguishes, separating while connecting) began disappearing as the national households took over, thereby abdicating freedom to necessity in the name of *le peuple,* the mass, a singular entity that obscures the inherent plurality of people in the world. Arendt's dissatisfaction with the social and the masses as categories basic to her understanding of the human condition predates in some ways the claim by Jean Baudrillard, an important figure in recent postmodern discourse, that the social, "that spongy referent" (1), is a fiction (with which she might agree) and that it no longer exists (with which she would not).

In 1972 (three years before her death), at a conference in Toronto on "The Work of Hannah Arendt," Arendt was asked for an example in our time of a social problem that is not at the same time a political problem in matters, say, of education, health, urban problems, or living standards. She replied that "with every one of these questions there is a double face. And one of these faces should not be subject to debate" ("OHA" 318). She believed that what can be figured out with certainty can be administered, but that what we cannot be certain about must be dealt with in public debate ("OHA" 317). Recently, Nancy Fraser in *Unruly Practices* understands the social as "a site of discourse about problematic needs" that have exceeded "the apparently (but not really) self-regulating domestic and official economic institutions of male-dominated, capitalist societies" (156). She argues that rather than having no genuinely political dimension, "needs are irreducibly interpretative," and that the social, rather than auguring the death of authentic politics, might be just the sphere for an "alternative socialist-feminist, dialogical mode of need interpretation" and a "participatory-democratic institutionalization of the social" (160 n. 32).

That same 1972 conference included an exchange—an accusation/challenge, fairly typical of her detractors, and her response—which is valuable to include here not to decide who is "right" but to show Arendt's approach to such issues. The challenge reads:

> It seems to me that one is forced to act politically, to deal with concrete situations and concrete problems. And insofar as one is forced to make those kinds of decisions then the question of class, the question of property, the question of the future of society becomes a very concrete problem and one can't anymore deal solely in terms of abstractions such as bureaucracy or abstractions such as centralization. These seem to me to reveal the basically de-politicized character of your thought which I found very disturbing when I read your work. Hearing you here today disturbs me even further, because fortunately—or unfortunately—we are forced to act in the world and we are going to have to know what the world looks like. ("OHA" 319)

Arendt's reply reads (in part):

> These are the problems of so-called "mass society." I say so-called "mass society" but it is unfortunately a fact. Now, I would like to know why you believe that words like class and property are less abstract than bureaucracy and administration or the words I use. They are exactly the same. All these belong to the same category of words. The question is only can you point to something very

real with these words. These words either have a revealing—or disclosing—quality or they haven't.

If you think that bureaucracy has no disclosing quality—which means the rule by the bureau,—then I believe you haven't really lived in the world long enough. But believe me bureaucracy is a reality much more so today than class. In other words, you use a number of abstract nouns which were once revealing, namely, in the nineteenth century, and you do not even bother to examine critically whether they still hold or whether they should be changed, or anything of that kind. ("OHA" 319–20)

The words that constitute ideas are all important to Arendt. They are what she thinks through and gives the history of. The disclosing quality of words is the key to the history of ideas. She insisted that "we must eventually come up against the phenomenon of language" when trying to deal with the past without the aid of tradition; "The Greek *polis* will continue to exist at the bottom of our political existence . . . for as long as we use the word 'politics'" (*MDT* 204). For Arendt, the word is the drill that plumbs the past, an idea that is close to Duras's sense of the power of words as a way of retrieving the past, of filtering experience. As Arendt wrote of Rahel, Goethe's "words freed her from the mute spell of sheer happening. And her ability to speak provided her with an *asylum* in the world" (see p. 113; my emphasis).

That, in the mind of a woman, language could be a safe harbor, a place of refuge, would indicate that although women come to language as exiles, without franked letters, without papers, they must assume the right of passage and become naturalized, become both insiders and outsiders. Women too must become conscious pariahs vis-à-vis the letter, the law. They must be able to insert themselves into the symbolic order so imbricated, although in a different register, in Arendt's notions of the public realm, the place where distance is maintained so that form and structure (relation) may appear from which meaning may be discerned, where abstraction—a loss of materiality (the body)—may not necessarily be a loss of difference.

As we learn from Lacan, to make a detour into psychoanalytic language, just because men have the organ, which makes it so easy for them to symbolize it, does not mean they have the phallus (*Ecrits: A Selection* 285), "the ultimate symbol of human Law in phallocratic societies" (Clément, *Lives and Legends* 132). According to Jane Gallop, Lacanians claim that neither sex can be or have the phallus (*Daughter's Seduction* 96). But, she warns:

> certainly the signifier "phallus" functions in distinction from "penis," but it always must refer to "penis." . . . Attempts to remake language according to one's own theoretical needs, as if language were merely a tool one could wield, is a very naive, un-Lacanian view of language [and an un-Arendtian view of language as well]. The question of whether one can separate "phallus" from "penis" rejoins the question of whether one can separate psychoanalysis from politics. . . . And as long as psychoanalysts maintain the separability of "phallus" from "penis," they can hold onto their "phallus" in the belief that their discourse has no relation to sexual inequality, no relation to politics. (*Daughter's Seduction* 97)

There are theoreticians, some female, who *do* separate "phallus" from "penis" without losing sight of the sexual politics involved in doing so.

Although I think these ideas illuminate Arendt's in the context of this study, I am not suggesting that she would have made much of a connection, if any at all, between discourse and sexual inequality or between psychoanalysis and politics. That the assumption of the phallus, "the cultural foundation of language" (Clément, *Lives and Legends* 180), is indeed an assumption of power, an endeavor in the masculine register, should not be avoided or denied by women so that sexual difference and distinction in general can be preserved. It should be assumed so that real heterogeneity can be fostered. Becoming a *maître-femme* (a master[ly]-woman) when necessary or desirable is a right and sometimes even a duty. Hence the relation of politics (which includes matters of sexual inequality) and language (in which sexual difference is constituted) appears in the public realm and is played and replayed on the terrain of that "second land," to recall Arendt's dream analysis (see p. 105). Freud on the subject of dreams called it "that other scene" (*ein andere Schauplatz*), which he designated as being the unconscious, whose effects, in Lacan's words, "are discovered at the level of the chain of materially unstable elements that constitute language" (*Ecrits: A Selection* 285).

Language makes the difference, and its hallmark is distance. The intervention of language separates, distances the psyche from itself, the child from its mother. It intervenes to prevent incest and obsessive love, and it keeps people from getting too close to (their) gods. Too much distance is also damaging. A person can be too far away to exercise the senses, to feel love or connection to others. As Clément puts it,

> the correct distance[3] exists: education, custom, law, civil society, and all of culture are there to maintain it, to preserve between individuals a relationship without the menace of [the absorption into the same, and the loss of the other]. (*Lives and Legends* 77)

But as she also points out, "the correct distance is the opposite of the feminine" (*Lives and Legends* 78). The feminine is generally understood to be close to, in an unmediated relation to, nature, emotions, and reality—lived experience.

Among feminists are many empiricists who believe that language can faithfully translate experience, that it (language) makes no difference. Such empiricism, "the science of experience" explains Alice Jardine, "is . . . that doctrine which holds that all knowledge originates in direct experience of what is commonly called reality, without theory, and undisturbed by language. That is, where language is superfluous to life" (*Gynesis* 151). For Arendt, being so close to "sheer happening" is to be "muted," " under a spell," and "freed" only by language—words (*RV* 115). Benjamin describes a difference between experience that is the "shock" of "the passing moment [*erlibnis*] in all its nakedness with no breath of prehistory [*mythos*] surround[ing] it" and a retrospective inward experience with an "aura" in the "magic of distance" (*Illuminations* 163–92).

Close to this idea is Arendt's notion of telling the story as the "mastering of a moment" in the past (see chapter 1, p. 16) that allows reconciliation, the understanding of events and actions. Such reconciliation can take place only with distance—precisely the element that Arendt privileges in her writing and her use of quotation. Language, words—writing especially—recognizes, invokes distance, that which is not feminine. Many women fear the loss of their experience in the distance that the letter promulgates (a fear that is not entirely unwarranted). An effort to minimize that distance (which can never be entirely eliminated) may be the reason that so much women's writing is done in a confessional mode, often in the form of thinly disguised autobiographical novels.

The desire behind confessional writing is not to translate experience (always already perceivable in language) but to try to deliver it unmarked by the letter itself. The illusion is that the confessional or heavily experiential writings keep the intimate safe from the symbolic, safe from abstraction and experimentation that falsifies, fractures, neuters, and assimilates that experience to itself. The effort amounts to a conscious refusal to be subjected to the letter (a virtual impossibility because it has already taken place and continues to do so on the level of the unconscious), which keeps experience particular, personal, and recognizable, and makes it a yardstick by which veracity, what is true, is measured. This insistence on experience turns this kind of feminism into the old humanism: representation, truth, and a clearly identified and identifiable subject (turning away from writing toward sociology).

In Arendt's stories, the reader can generalize without falsifying, invoke difference and distinction by thinking through the words by which we try to understand the past, the world. The question this study is exploring, the relation of experience and experiment, does not reside in an opposition between experience and experiment (to widen the parameters somewhat, one may read the opposition as between sociology and writing or may even see it in terms of its practitioners, as in Elaine Marks's illuminating nomination of two kinds of women writers, "data gatherers *or* text rubbers" ["Feminisms Wake" 96]). It results rather in both/and, experience and experiment—in relation to one another.

For Arendt, the writing itself finds experience—its trace must be there. It is a way of telling the past, of finding (out) what will have been the future, of writing between past and future. As she wrote so typically in her famous "Home to Roost" address in Boston on the occasion of the bicentennial (one of her last—she died six months later at the age of sixty-nine):

> I rather believe with Faulkner, "The past is never dead, it is not even past," and this for the simple reason that the world we live in at any moment *is* the world of the past; it consists of the monuments and the relics of what has been done by men for better or worse; its facts are always what has become (as the Latin origin of the word: *fieri-factum est* suggest). In other words, it is quite true that the past *haunts* us; it is the past's function to haunt us who are present and wish to live in the world as it really is, that is, has *become* what it is now. (6)

Arendt's scene of writing is not the construction of theories, not writing the body, but writing the world—a world that is always already written but must be (re)discovered with each writing. The telling of stories may put Arendt on the threshold of the poststructural, postmodern condition.[4] Here my own errantry through Arendt's work, wandering between private and public, pariah and parvenu, past and future, meets such a horizon—a space, perhaps where three roads meet, freedom, feminism, and postmodernism, three roads that not unreasonably suggest the trivium: grammar, rhetoric, and logic; that is, language as the point of intersection, coupled with the Oedipal desire to pose the questions and elicit answers.

Arendt was not interested in systematizing her thought into theoretical formulations. She believed that although thinking could influence action, theory did not. It could only do so in the reform of consciousness, which, because of the number of consciousnesses that would have to be reformed, was tantamount to impossible. This insistence on the concrete notion of "mankind" as a plurality, not an image of a single individual, remained constant throughout her life and in her work. She believed that acting is often done in concert with others and that thinking is a matter for each individual. She was not willing to indoctrinate or proselytize.

> I cannot tell you black on white—and would hate to do it—what consequences of this kind of thought which I try, not to indoctrinate, but to rouse or to awaken in my students, are, in actual politics. I can very well imagine that one becomes a republican and a third a liberal or God knows what. ("OHA" 309)

Arendt did hope, though, that by her example of thinking, "certain extreme things which are the consequences of non-thinking . . . will not be capable [of arising]" ("OHA" 309). Among the extreme things she refers to are the events of the holocaust, namely, the activities of Adolph Eichmann. Her book *Eichmann in Jerusalem,* originally a five-part article for *The New Yorker,* is an account of his trial, which caused a great furor among Jews everywhere, but especially in the United States and Israel. Arendt—accused of being cold and soulless, and by some, even of being anti-Semitic—was virtually excommunicated by the Jewish intellectual community for indicting Jewish functionaries or councils (*Judenrate*) for cooperating, under duress, with the Nazis during the "Final Solution," especially after 1941. In answer to Gershom Scholem (a scholar of Jewish history and mysticism, and a close friend to Benjamin), who wrote a scathing letter accusing her of lacking *Herzenstakt* (sympathy) for her own people and denouncing her book for the inappropriate "flippancy" of its tone, she wrote:

> I said that there was no possibility of resistance [on the part of the Jews], but there existed the possibility of *doing nothing*. . . . Since we are dealing in politics with men, and not with heroes or saints, it is this possibility of "*nonparticipation*" (Kircheimer) that is decisive if we begin to judge, not the system, but the individual, his choices and his arguments. (Letter to Scholem, Feldman 249)

Also in *Eichmann in Jerusalem,* Arendt, always rethinking her words and the ideas they disclose, restates her notion of evil, which did not sit well with many. In the earlier *Origins of Totalitarianism* (published in 1951), Arendt spoke of a "radical evil" of which it is

> inherent in our entire philosophical tradition that we cannot conceive. . . . we actually have nothing we can fall back on in order to understand a phenomenon that nevertheless confronts us with its overpowering reality and breaks down all the standards we know. (3:157)

Some thirteen years later, in the Eichmann book, whose subtitle is *A Report on the Banality of Evil,* Arendt reversed herself (as she had done on other occasions), saying that

> evil is never "radical," . . . it is only extreme . . . it possesses neither depth nor demonic dimension. It can overgrow and lay waste the whole world precisely because it spreads like a fungus on the surface. It is "thought-defying" as I said [the last words of the last chapter of *Eichmann in Jerusalem* are "word-and-thought-defying *banality of evil*" (252)] because thought tries to reach some depth, to go to the roots, and the moment it concerns itself with evil, it is frustrated because there is nothing. That is its "banality." Only the good has depth and can be radical. (Letter to Scholem, Feldman 251)

Arendt's definition of banal is strict. It means commonplace, not commonly occurring. She was adamant that Eichmann was not Everyman ("OHA" 308). To her, this banal man was the typical parvenu. He wanted only the approval of those he obeyed. He had no conscience to interfere with this behavior (which is not the same as acting). His conscience spoke only the platitudes of the Nazi "respectability" he sought to wrap himself in. Much of Arendt's characterization of Eichmann was construed as trivializing the man and his deeds. Most wanted to see him as a hideous monster rather than a thoughtless nonentity.

Finally, Arendt stated that she thought an international tribunal, not a Jewish one, should have sat in judgment of Eichmann because his crime was not just a crime against the Jews but a crime against humanity. Her reasons for her conclusions are exemplary of the careful attention she gives to the words she uses.

> Had the court in Jerusalem understood that there were distinctions between discrimination, expulsion, and genocide, it would immediately have become clear that the supreme crime it was confronted with, the physical extermination of the Jewish people, was a crime against humanity, perpetrated upon the body of the Jewish people, and that only the choice of victims, not the nature of the crime, could be derived from the long history of Jew-hatred and anti-Semitism. Insofar as the victims were Jews, it was right and proper that a Jewish court should sit in judgment; but insofar as the crime was a crime against humanity, it needed an international tribunal to do justice to it. (*EJ* 269)

Young-Bruehl reports that much of *Eichmann in Jerusalem*'s reception consisted of

> comments about Jews with death wishes, Jews incapable of resistance, victims as responsible for their own executions [all of which] accrued to Arendt's remarks about the Jewish councils' actions. Charges that she was anti-Israel, anti-Zionist, a Jewish self-hater, a legal purist, a Kantian moralist accompanied Arendt's reflections on the legal precedents of the trial and questions of international law. (337)

Once again Arendt proved herself a pariah within the *pariahvolk.* Her judgments, her understandings, were plainly the result only of her thinking through the issues as she put them down in words on paper. "The writing is somehow a *cura posterior* for me," (Young-Bruehl 374)—a later reflection, a postwriting. It is interesting and important to note the range (and clustering) of words given in my *New College Latin Dictionary* as meanings for *cura*—nearly all of which are, in one degree or another, apropos:

> care, concern, worry; care, pains, attention; heartache; object of concern; sweetheart; administration, management, charge; trusteeship, guardianship; means of healing, cure, treatment; guardian, keeper; study, reflection; literary effort, literary work.

From "care, concern" to "literary work" is the road Arendt traveled as she embraced the tradition of *amor mundi,* a concept she held onto, sometimes for dear life, as she herself suffered the ignominy, the exile and statelessness, imposed by the Nazi juggernaut and its aftermath. With this *cura posterior,* she was able to begin to immerse herself more in *la vita contemplativa* that she had had to give up for *la vita activa,* for world history and politics, and to prepare the way for her most philosophical text, *The Life of the Mind.*

That Arendt was a Jew, doubly other, probably did not consciously or ordinarily enter her thinking as a discrete factor. An active forgetting could be at work in this. As she had put it once, she was quite used to being a woman, having been one all her life (see chapter 1, p. 12). She had also been a Jew that same amount of time and was quite used to that as well. Her response to Scholem's letter criticizing her so severely for *Eichmann in Jerusalem* somehow managed, however, to tease the connection between her being both a Jew and a woman out of her unconscious:

> I found it puzzling that you should write "I regard you wholly as a daughter of our people, and in no other way." The truth is I have never pretended to be anything else or to be in any other way than I am, and I have never even felt tempted in that direction. *It would have been like saying that I was a man and not a woman—that is to say, kind of insane.* (Letter to Scholem, Feldman 246; my emphasis)

Here, being both a Jew and a woman is thoroughly enmeshed, the one undeniable on the basis of the other.[5] Such unconscious revelations and connections hook up with that horizon that bespeaks experiment, a horizon that may border on the postmodern. The open-endedness inherent in such a horizon resides also in Jewish thought, in which there is no fulfillment of the word.[6]

For Arendt there are no utopias, no master-narratives, no promises. Rather, the writing—or, as she might see it, the stories—articulates that somewhat intangible space that lies between—*inter-est*—people.

Notes

Chapter 1

The chapter title is a line from Gertrude Stein's essay "What is English Literature" (*Look at Me Now* 32).

1. Although relatively little has been written about experimental women writers of fiction, some recent critical and theoretical texts are of interest. Suleiman discusses some of the women connected to the surrealist movement who, while mainly known (if at all) as artists, were also avant-garde writers. Her *Subversive Intent* contributes a great deal to the infrequently discussed relation of women artists to experiment and experimental movements, including postmodernism at the end of the book; she also has sections on Duras and Winterson. Friedman and Fuchs's *Breaking the Chain* provides a short history of experimental women writers and critical analyses of various texts. In recent years, most of the emphasis on women in postmodern literary work has been placed on the issue of inclusivity. Among those texts are De Lauretis, *Technologies of Gender;* Trinh, *Woman, Native, Other* (Trinh also writes about Duras); and Owens, "The Discourse of Others: Feminism and Postmodernism." Hutcheon on postmodernism, Butler on gender identity, and Caughie on Woolf and postmodernism are also illuminating.

2. Of special interest concerning the relation of women to modernism is Huyssen's idea (in *After the Great Divide*) that the Masses, despised by modernists, are coded as feminine.

3. Arendt had not given up using the generic *men* or *man* or masculine pronouns to indicate mixed or unspecified referents. I had little objection to this at first, ascribing such a mannerism to a generational difference. As time went on, however, and my reading of her work took on a greater intensity and insistence in my own, I became increasingly aware of and uncomfortable with a persistent masculine presence in her writing that had long since gone out of my own. Because of this, I found myself retaining her usage when I quote her and using alternatives in my commentary.

4. The phrase is Rahel Varnhagen's, as quoted by Arendt in *RV* 206.

5. It is interesting to note that in *Gates of Ivory,* her latest novel, Drabble

has included a bibliography on the issues and events she is concerned with in the story.

6. The following are the quoted passages by Gauthier, Foucault, and Cixous (respectively) in the original French (the translations in the text are mine).

Je sais que, quand je lis vos livres [ceux de Duras], ça me met dans un état très . . . , très fort et je suis très mal à l'aise et c'est très difficile de parler ou de faire quelque chose, après les avoir lus. (Duras and Gauthier 15)

La lecture [de Duras] que j'en ai fait . . . me laissent toujours une impression très fort. La présence de l'oeuvre de Marguerite Duras reste très intense . . . et puis voilà qu'au moment d'en parler, j'ai l'impression que tout m'échappe. Une espèce de force nue contre laquelle on vient glisser, sur laquelle les mains n'ont pas de prise. C'est la présence de cette force, cette force mobile et lisse, de cette présence en même temps fuyante, c'est ça qui m'empêche d'en parler, et qui sans doute m'attache à elle. (Foucault and Cixous 8)

J'ai repris tous les textes de Marguerite Duras, que j'ai lus plusieurs fois, et dont je me disais, naïvement: je les connais bien. Or on ne peux pas connaître Marguerite Duras, on ne peut pas la saisir. Je me dis: je connais, j'ai lu, et je m'aperçois que je n'ai pas "retenu." C'est peut être ça: il y a un effet Duras et cet effet Duras c'est que quelque chose s'écoule qui est très puissant. . . . Elle m'appris quelque chose qui dépasse presque le texte bien que ce soit un effet d'écriture quant à un certain épanchement. (Foucault and Cixous 8–9)

7. Unless otherwise indicated, all translations are mine.

8. For an astute reading of the relation of Duras, the author, and Jacques Hold, her narrator, in *Le ravissement de Lol V. Stein,* see Sulieman 110–18.

9. *Oxford Dictionary of English of Etymology,* 3d ed.

Chapter 2

1. For discussion of some of the accidents or chance occurrences in Drabble's work, see Harper, especially 159 and 165.

2. See Hassan, *The Dismemberment of Orpheus,* especially 269–70.

3. See Alan Wilde, 15, 188, and passim.

4. Harper makes a convincing case for Drabble as a postmodern writer by demonstrating her refusal to comply with the tenets of high modernist art and her interest in developing her reputation as a writer rather than an artist. For these reasons, she has allowed and even perpetuated the myth that she is an old-fashioned writer. Harper provides a review of Drabble's critical reception.

5. Historical references in this paragraph are from *The New Encyclopedia Britannica,* 15th ed.

6. *New Encyclopedia Britannica,* 15th ed.

7. According to Michèle Montrelay, a concentricity in feminine sexuality organized around Jones's archaic vaginal-oral schema constitutes what he calls precocious femininity. The pun in my text plays on this notion of a concentric female sexual economy as opposed to the phallocentric; concentricity, then, is a feminine configuration, and its prefix *con* further reinforces this notion of "woman-centeredness" because *con* is French for cunt.

8. *American Heritage Dictionary,* 2d ed. (Boston: Houghton Mifflin, 1982).

9. The phrase is Frederic Jameson's. See "Imaginary and Symbolic in Lacan," 353.

10. According to Derrida, the Greek word for apocalypse comes from the Hebrew *gala* ("Of an Apocalyptic Tone" 64).

Chapter 3

1. Richard Seaver has translated *Le ravissement de Lol V. Stein* as *The Ravishing of Lol Stein.* Inexplicably he leaves out the letter *V* from Lol's name in the title and throughout the book. Moreover, he converts all the letters in Duras's text to full names: S. Thala becomes South Thala, U. Bridge becomes Uxbridge, and T. Beach becomes Town Beach. Duras's lettered text, a text full of letters, is, in his hands, emptied of letters entirely. The repetition of the letters, especially the *V* in the name, is central to my reading of Duras's text; leaving them out is a grave error.

2. *Le jeu de la mourre* is the paper/scissors/stone guessing game in which the three elements indicated by a show of fingers can dominate, in turn, the *jeu de la mourre.*

3. For a development of the concepts of the insistence of the letter and of the *H* as the letter of separation, see Lydon, "Story of Adèle H." 33–41.

4. The relation of *graft* and *graph* is developed by Jacques Derrida in several of his texts, including "La double séance," where he considers not only the etymolgical coincidence between the two words but the analogy between the forms of textual grafting and vegetal grafting. For an extremely useful synthesis of the graft in Derrida's work, see Jonathan Culler's section "Grafts and Graft" in his *On Deconstruction.*

5. K refers to the Kilmartin revision of the C. K. Scott Moncrieff translation of *A la recherche du temps perdu* published in 1981. See Moncrieff for the complete reference.

6. See also Lydon, "Translating Duras" 261, for some remarks on these issues.

Chapter 4

1. Among them was Martin Heidegger, whose seminars she attended at Marburg in 1922–23. They were estranged for some seventeen years, until a reunion in 1949, and although she contributed to a birthday festschrift for him ("Martin Heidegger at Eighty") and made efforts to understand his political

failures before, during, and after the war, privately she was much more critical of him than she ever admitted publicly, as Young-Bruehl has shown (442–45).

2. See Derrida, "Women in the Beehive" 197–203.

3. Clément refers to Lévi-Strauss's discovery of the valuable notion of a correct distance between tribes held by the Mandan Indians of North America: the tribes must not be so close as to create friction and hostility and must not be so far as to become strangers and enemies in war. Notions of the correct distance are germane to Lacan's work and to Clément's discussion of Lacan in her *Lives and Legends of Jacques Lacan*.

4. See Philip Lewis, especially 23.

5. Hélène Cixous conflates the two in her neologism *Jewoman* (in French, *juifemme*), which has a different emphasis and a different tone from the old, self-effacing pejorative *Jewess*. Cixous's neologism signals a more global and lapidary usage: all women are inevitably Jews.

6. See Handelman, especially 90.

Bibliography

Abel, Elizabeth, ed. *Writing and Sexual Difference.* 1980, 1981. Chicago: U of Chicago P, 1982.

Ames, Sanford S. "Cinderella's Slipper: Mallarmé's Letters in Duras." *Visible Language* 12.3 (1978): 245–254.

———. "Edging the Shadow: Duras from Hiroshima to Beaubourg."

Ames, *Remains to Be Seen* 3–30.

———, ed. *Remains to Be Seen: Essays on Marguerite Duras.* New York: Peter Lang, 1988.

Arendt, Hannah. "The Archimedean Point." *Ingenor,* College of Engineering, U of Michigan (Spring 1969): 4–9, 24–26.

———. *Between Past and Future: Eight Exercises in Political Thought.* 1968. New York: Penguin, 1977.

———. *Crises of the Republic.* New York: Harcourt, 1972.

———. *Eichmann in Jerusalem: A Report on the Banality of Evil.* Rev. ed. New York: Viking, 1964.

———. "Home to Roost: A Bicentennial Address." *New York Review of Books* 26 June 1975: 3–6.

———. *The Human Condition.* Chicago: U of Chicago P, 1958.

———. "The Jew as Pariah: A Hidden Tradition." Feldman 67–90.

———. *Lectures on Kant's Political Philosoy.* Ed. Ronald Beiner. Chicago: U of Chicago P, 1982.

———. *The Life of the Mind.* 1977, 1978. New York: Harcourt, 1981.

———. *Love and St. Augustine: An Essay in Philosophical Interpretation.* Trans. by E. B. Ashton of her Ph. D. diss., *Der Liebes begriffe bei Augustin.* Berlin: J. Springer, 1929.

———. "Martin Heidegger at Eighty." *Heidegger and Modern Philosophy: Critical Essays.* Ed. Michael Murray. New Haven: Yale UP, 1978.

———. *Men in Dark Times.* New York: Harcourt, 1968.

———. "Nathalie Sarraute." *New York Review of Books* 5 March 1964: 5–6.

———. "On Hannah Arendt." Hill, *Hannah Arendt* 301–40.

———. *On Revolution.* 1965. New York: Pelican, 1977.

———. *The Origins of Totalitarianism.* 3 vols. 1951. New York: Harcourt, 1968.

————. *Rahel Varnhagen: Lebensgeschichte einer deutschen Judin aus der Romantik.* Munich: Piper, 1959.

————. *Rahel Varnhagen: The Life of a Jewish Woman.* Trans. Richard and Clara Winston. Rev. ed. New York: Harcourt, 1974.

————. "Understanding and Politics." *Partisan Review* 20.4 (July–August 1953): 377–92.

Barthes, Roland. *Critical Essays.* Evanston: Northwestern UP, 1972.

————. *Image, Music, Text.* Trans. Stephen Heath. New York: Hill and Wang, 1977.

————. *The Pleasure of the Text.* Trans. Richard Miller. New York: Hill and Wang, 1974.

————. *Roland Barthes on Roland Barthes.* Trans. Richard Howard. New York: Hill and Wang, 1977.

————. "To Write: An Intransitive Verb?" *The Structuralist Controversy: The Languages of Criticism and the Sciences of the Mind.* Ed. Richard Macksey and Eugenio Donato. Baltimore: Johns Hopkins U P, 1972. 134–45.

Baudrillard, Jean. *In the Shadow of the Silent Majorities . . . or The End of the Social and Other Essays.* Trans. Paul Foss, Paul Patton, and John Johnston. New York: Semiotext(e), 1983.

Beauvoir, Simone de. *The Second Sex.* Trans. and ed. H. M. Parshley. 1952. New York: Vintage, 1974.

Beckett, Samuel. "Imagination Dead Imagine." *First Love and Other Shorts.* New York: Grove, 1974.

————. *Proust.* New York: Grove, 1957.

Bedford, Sybille. "Emancipation and Destiny." Rev. of *Rahel Varnhagen: The Life of a Jewess,* by Hannah Arendt. *The Reconstructionist* 12 December 1958: 22–26.

————. *A Legacy.* New York: Simon and Schuster, 1957.

Benjamin, Walter. *Illuminations.* Ed. and intro. Hannah Arendt. Trans. Harry Zohn. New York: Schocken, 1969.

Blau, Herbert. *The Eye of Prey: Subversions of the Postmodern.* Bloomington: Indiana UP, 1987.

Bloom, Harold. *The Anxiety of Influence: A Theory of Poetry.* New York: Oxford UP, 1973.

Boethius, Anicius Manlius Severinus. *The Consolation of Philosophy.* Trans. I. T. Ed. and intro. William Anderson. Carbondale: Southern Illinois UP, 1963.

Bromberg, Pamela S. "Narrative on Drabble's *The Middle Ground:* Relativity versus Teleology." *Contemporary Literature* 24.4 (Winter 1983): 463–79.

Brooke-Rose, Christine. "Illiterations." Friedman and Fuchs, 55–71.

Burke, Carolyn. "Irigaray through the Looking Glass." *Feminist Studies* 72.2 (Summer 1981): 288–304.

————. "Report from Paris: Women's Writing and the Women's Movement." *Signs* 3.4 (1978): 843–55.

Burke, Kenneth. *A Grammar of Motives.* Berkeley: U of California P, 1969.

Butler, Judith. *Gender Trouble: Feminism and the Subversion of Identity.* New York: Routledge, 1990.

Butor, Michel. "La critique et l'invention." *Répertoire*. 5 vols. Paris: Minuit, 1968. 3:7–20. Trans. Mary Lydon. "Criticism and Invention." *Cream City Review* 8.1–2 (1983): 1–12.

———. *Inventory: Essays by Michel Butor*. Trans. Richard Howard. New York: Simon and Schuster, 1968.

Callahan, Anne. "Vagabondage: Duras." Ames, *Remains to Be Seen* 197–203.

Caughie, Pamela. *Virginia Woolf & Postmodernism: Literature in Quest & Question of Itself*. Urbana: U of Illinois P, 1991.

Cherchez La Femme: Feminist Critique/Feminine Text. Ed. Cynthia Chase, Nelly Furman, and Mary Jacobus. *Diacritics* 12.2 (Summer 1982): special issue.

Cismaru, Alfred. *Marguerite Duras*. New York: Twayne, 1971.

Cixous, Hélène. "The Laugh of the Medusa." Trans. Keith Cohen and Paula Cohen. Marks and Courtivron 245–64.

Cixous, Hélène, and Catherine Clément. *La jeune née*. Paris: Union générale d'éditions, 1979. Trans. Betsy Wing. *The Newly Born Woman*. Intro. Sandra M. Gilbert. Minneapolis: U of Minnesota P, 1986.

Clément, Catherine. *The Lives and Legends of Jacques Lacan*. Trans. Arthur Goldhammer. New York: Columbia UP, 1983.

Cooper-Clark, Diana. "Margaret Drabble: Cautious Feminist." Rose, *Critical Essays* 19–30.

Culler, Jonathan. *On Deconstruction: Theory and Criticism after Deconstruction*. Ithaca: Cornell UP, 1982.

de Lauretis, Teresa. *Alice Doesn't: Feminism, Semiotics, Cinema*. Bloomington: Indiana UP, 1984.

———. *Technologies of Gender: Essays on Theory, Film, and Fiction*. Bloomington: Indiana UP, 1987.

Defoe, Daniel. *Robinson Crusoe*. New York: Modern Library, 1948.

Derrida, Jacques. *Dissemination*. Trans. Barbara Johnson. Chicago: U of Chicago P, 1982.

———. "La double séance." *La Dissemination*. Paris: Seuil, 1972. Trans. Barbara Johnson. "The Double Session." *Dissemination*. Chicago: U of Chicago P, 1982.

———. "Freud and the Scene of Writing." *YFS* 48 (1972): 74–117.

———. "Of an Apocalyptic Tone Recently Adopted in Philosophy." Trans. John P. Leavey, Jr. *Semeia* 23 (1982): 63–97.

———. *Of Grammatology*. Trans. and intro. Gayatri Chakravorty Spivak. Baltimore: Johns Hopkins UP, 1976.

———. "The Parergon." Trans. Craig Owens. *October* 9 (1979): 3–40.

———. "The Purveyor of Truth." *YFS* 52 (1975): 31–114.

———. *Spurs*. Trans. Barbara Harlow. Chicago: U of Chicago P, 1978.

———. "Women in the Beehive: A Seminar with Jacques Derrida." Jardine and Smith 189–203.

———. *Writing and Difference*. Trans. Alan Bass. Chicago: U of Chicago P, 1978.

Derrida, Jacques, and Christie V. McDonald. "Choreographies." *Diacritics* 12.2 (Summer 1982): 66–76.

Descombes, Vincent. *Modern French Philosophy*. Trans. L. Scott-Fox and J. M. Harding. 1980. Cambridge, Eng.: Cambridge UP, 1982.

Diamond, Arlyn, and Lee R. Edwards. *The Authority of Experience*. Amherst: U of Massachusetts P, 1977.

Dickinson, Emily. *The Complete Poems of Emily Dickinson*. Ed. Thomas H. Johnson. Boston: Little, Brown, 1960.

Dillard, Annie. *Living by Fiction*. 1982. New York: Harper, 1983.

Drabble, Margaret. *The Gates of Ivory*. New York: Viking, 1991.

———. *The Ice Age*. New York: Knopf, 1977.

———. *Jerusalem the Golden*. 1967. New York: Popular Library, 1967.

———. *The Middle Ground*. New York: Knopf, 1980.

———. *A Natural Curiosity*. New York: Viking, 1989.

———. *The Needle's Eye*. 1972. New York: Knopf, 1977.

———. *The Radiant Way*. New York: Knopf, 1987.

———. *The Realms of Gold*. London: Weidenfeld and Nicolson, 1975.

———. *A Summer Bird-Cage*. 1964. New York: Popular Library, 1977.

———. *The Waterfall*. 1969. New York: Popular Library, 1977.

Draenos, Stan Spyros. "Thinking without a Ground: Hannah Arendt and the Contemporary Situation of Understand-ing." Hill, *Hannah Arendt* 209–24.

Dupuy, Jean-Pierre. *Ordres et désordres: Pour un nouveau paradigm*. Paris: Seuil, 1982.

Duras, Marguerite. *Abahn Sabana David*. Paris: Gallimard, 1970.

———. *Agatha*. Paris: Minuit, 1981.

———. *L'amant*. Paris: Minuit, 1984. Trans. Barbara Bray. *The Lover*. New York: Pantheon, 1985.

———. *L'amante anglaise*. Paris: Gallimard, 1967. Trans. Barbara Bray. London: Hamish Hamilton, 1968.

———. *L'amour*. Paris: Gallimard, 1971.

———. *L'après-midi de Monsieur Andesmas*. Paris: Gallimard, 1962.

———. "Aurélia Steiner." *Le navire Night* 139–66.

———. *Un barrage contre le Pacific*. Paris: Gallimard, 1950. Trans. Antonia White. *A Sea of Troubles*. London: Methuen, 1953.

———. *Le Camion suivi de entretien avec Michelle Porte*. Paris: Minuit, 1977.

———. *Détruire dit-elle*. Paris: Minuit, 1969. Trans. Barbara Bray. *Destroy, She Said and Destruction and Language: An Interview with Marguerite Duras*. Trans. Helen Lane Cumberford. New York: Grove, 1970.

———. *La douleur*. Paris: P.O.L., 1985. Trans. Barbara Bray. *The War: A Memoir*. New York: Pantheon, 1986.

———. *L'Eden Cinéma*. Paris: Mercure, 1977.

———. *Four Novels: The Square, Moderato Cantabile, Ten-Thirty on a Summer Night, The Afternoon of Mr. Andesmas*. New York: Grove, 1965.

———. *Hiroshima mon amour: Scénario and dialogue*. Réalisation, Alain Resnais. Paris: Gallimard, 1960. Trans. Richard Seaver. *Hiroshima Mon Amour: Text by Marguerite Duras for the film by Alain Resnais*. Picture Editor, Robert Hughes. New York: Grove, 1961.

———. *India Song: Texte théâtre film*. Paris: Gallimard, 1973. Trans. Barbara Bray. *India Song*. New York: Grove, 1976.

———. *La maladie de la mort*. Paris: Minuit, 1982. Trans. Barbara Bray. *The Malady of Death*. New York: Grove, 1986.

———. *Marguerite Duras*. Paris: Albatros, 1979. Trans. Edith Cohen and Peter Conner. *Marguerite Duras by Marguerite Duras*. San Francisco: City Lights, 1987.

———. *Marguerite Duras à Montréal: Textes réunis et présentés par Suzanne Lamy et André Roy*. Montreal, Editions Spirale, 1981.

———. *Moderato Cantabile suivi de Moderato Cantabile et la presse française*. Paris: Minuit, 1958.

———. *Le navire Night, Cesarée, les mains negatives, Aurélia Steiner, Aurélia Steiner, Aurélia Steiner*. Paris: Mercure, 1982.

———. *Nathalie Granger suivi de La femme du Ganges*. Paris: Gallimard, 1973.

———. *Outside: Papiers d'un jour*. Paris: P.O.L., 1984. Trans. Arthur Goldhammer. *Outside: Selected Writings*. Boston: Beacon, 1986.

———. *Les petits chevaux de Tarquinia*. Paris: Gallimard, 1953. Trans. Peter DuBerg. *The Little Horses of Tarquinia*. London: Calder, 1960.

———. *Le ravissement de Lol V. Stein*. Paris: Gallimard, 1964. Trans. Richard Seaver. *The Ravishing of Lol Stein*. New York: Grove, 1966.

———. *Savannah Bay*. Paris: Minuit, 1983.

———. *Le vice-consul*. Paris: Gallimard, 1966. Trans. Eileen Ellenbogen. *The Vice-Consul*. London: Hamish Hamilton, 1968.

———. *Les yeux verts*. Spec. issue of *Cahiers du Cinéma* 312/313 (1980).

Duras, Marguerite, and Michelle Porte. *Les lieux de Marguerite Duras*. Paris: Minuit, 1977.

Duras, Marguerite, and Xavière Gauthier. *Les parleuses*. Paris: Minuit, 1974. Trans. Katherine A. Jensen. *Woman to Woman*. Lincoln: U of Nebraska P, 1987.

"'Eichmann in Jerusalem': An Exchange of Letters between Gershom Scholem and Hannah Arendt." Feldman 240–51.

Eisenstein, Hester, and Alice Jardine, eds. *The Future of Difference*. Boston: G. K. Hall, 1980.

Federman, Raymond, ed. *Surfiction: Fiction Now . . . and Tomorrow*. 2nd ed. Chicago: Swallow, 1981.

———. "What Are Experimental Novels and Why Are There So Many Left Unread?" *Genre* 14.1 (Spring 1981): 23–31.

Feldman, Ron H., ed. *The Jew as Pariah: Jewish Identity and Politics in the Modern Age*. New York: Grove, 1978.

Felman, Shoshana. "Madness and Philosophy or Literature's Reason." *YFS* 52 (1975): 206–28.

———. "Turning the Screw of Interpretation." *YFS* 55/56 (1977): 94-207.

———. "Woman and Madness: The Critical Phallacy." *Diacritics* 5.4 (Winter 1975): 2–10.

Feminist Readings: French Texts/American Contexts. Ed. Collette Gaudin et al. Spec. issue of *YFS* 62 (1981).

Foster, Hal, ed. *The Anti-Aesthetic: Essays on Postmodern Culture*. Port Townsend, WA: Bay, 1983.

Foucault, Michel. *Language, Counter-Memory, Practice: Selected Essays and Interviews*. Ed. and intro. Donald F. Bouchard. Trans. Donald F. Bouchard and Sherry Simon. Ithaca: Cornell UP, 1977.

Foucault, Michel, and Hélène Cixous. "A Propos de Marguerite Duras." *Cahier Renaud-Barrault* 89 (October 1975): 8–22.

Fraser, Nancy. *Unruly Practices: Power, Discourse, and Gender in Contemporary Social Theory*. Minneapolis: U of Minnesota P, 1989.

Freud, Sigmund. "'The Antithetical Sense of Primal Words.'" Nelson 55–62.

———. *Beyond the Pleasure Principle*. Trans. James Strachey. New York: Norton, 1961.

———. "Femininity." *New Introductory Lectures*. Trans. James Strachey. New York: Norton, 1965, 1964.

———. "Fetishism." *Sexuality and the Psychology of Love*. Ed. Philip Rieff. New York: Collier, 1963.

———. *The Interpretation of Dreams*. Trans. James Strachey. New York: Avon, 1965.

———. *Jokes and Their Relation to the Unconscious*. Trans. James Strachey. New York: Norton, 1969.

———. "Note upon the Mystic Writing Pad." *General Psychological Theory: Papers on Metapsychology*. Ed. and intro. Philip Rieff. New York: Collier, 1963.

———. *The Psychopathology of Everyday Life*. Trans. Alan Tyson. Ed. and intro. James Strachey. New York: Norton, 1965.

———. "The Relation of the Poet to Daydreaming." Nelson 44–55.

———. *Sexuality and the Psychology of Love*. Ed. Philip Rieff. New York: Collier, 1963.

———. "The Theme of the Three Caskets." Nelson 63–75.

———. "The Uncanny." Nelson 122–61.

Friedman, Ellen G., and Miriam Fuchs, eds. *Breaking the Sequence: Women's Experimental Fiction*. Princeton: Princeton UP, 1989.

Frye, Northrup. *Anatomy of Criticism: Four Essays*. Princeton: Princeton UP, 1957.

Furman, Nelly. "Textual Feminism." McConnell-Ginet, Borker, and Furman 45–54.

Gallop, Jane. "Critical Response to *Writing and Sexual Difference:* The Difference Within." Abel 283–90.

———. *The Daughter's Seduction: Feminism and Psychoanalysis*. Ithaca: Cornell UP, 1982.

———. "Quand nos lèvres s'écrivent: Irigaray's Body Politic." *Romanic Review* 74.1 (January 1983): 77–83.

Gilbert, Sandra. "What Do Feminist Critics Want? Or a Postcard from the Volcano." *ADE Bulletin* 66 (Winter 1980): 16–24.

Gilbert, Sandra, and Susan Gubar. *Madwoman in the Attic*. New Haven: Yale UP, 1979.

Goodman, Kay. "Poesis and Praxis in Rahel Varnhagen's Letters." *New German Critique* 27 (Fall 1982): 123–40.

Gray, Francine du Plessix. "The War." Rev. of *The War,* by Marguerite Duras. *New York Times Book Review* 4 May 1986: 1, 48.

Greve, Ludwig. "Hannah Arendt." *Partisan Review* 46.2 (1979): 317–18.

Gussow, Mel. "Margaret Drabble: A Double Life." *New York Times Book Review* 9 October 1977: 7, 40–41.

Handelman, Susan. *The Slayers of Moses: The Emergence of Rabbinic Interpretation in Modern Literary Theory.* Albany: State U of New York P, 1982.

Hardwick, Elizabeth. *Sleepless Nights.* New York: Random House, 1979.

Harper, Michael F. "Margaret Drabble and the Resurrection of the English Novel." *Contemporary Literature* 23.2 (1982): 145–68.

Hassan, Ihab. *The Dismemberment of Orpheus: Toward a Postmodern Literature.* 2nd ed. Madison: U of Wisconsin P, 1982.

Heath, Stephen. *The Nouveau Roman: A Study in the Practice of Writing.* Philadelphia: Temple UP, 1972.

———. "Difference." *Screen* 9.4 (Winter 1978/79): 51–112.

Heidegger, Martin. *Early Greek Thinking.* Trans. David Farrell Krell and Frank A. Capuzzi. New York: Harper, 1975.

Hill, Melvin A., ed. *Hannah Arendt: The Recovery of the Public World.* New York: St. Martin's, 1979.

Homans, Margaret. "'Her Very Own Howl': The Ambiguities of Representation in Recent Women's Fiction." *Signs* 9 (1983): 186–205.

———. *Women Writers and Poetic Identity: Dorothy Wordsworth, Emily Brontë, and Emily Dickinson.* Princeton: Princeton UP, 1980.

Howard, Maureen. "Public and Private Games." Rev. of *The Ice Age,* by Margaret Drabble. *New York Times Book Review* 9 October 1977: 7, 40.

Husserl-Kapit, Susan. "An Interview with Marguerite Duras." *Signs* 1.2 (1975): 423–34.

Hutcheon, Linda. "A Poetics of Postmodernism?" *Diacritics* 13.4 (Winter 1983): 33–42.

———. *A Poetics of Postmodernism: History, Theory, Fiction.* New York: Routledge, 1988.

———. "Subject in/of/to History and His Story." *Diacritics* 16.1 (Spring 1986): 78–91.

Huyssen, Andreas. *After the Great Divide.* Bloomington: Indiana UP, 1986.

Irigaray, Luce. *Speculum of the Other Woman.* Trans. Gillian C. Gill. Ithaca: Cornell UP, 1985.

———. *This Sex Which Is Not One.* Trans. Catherine Porter with Carolyn Burke. Ithaca: Cornell UP, 1985.

Jacobus, Mary. "The Difference of View." Jacobus et al. 10–12.

Jacobus, Mary, et al. *Women Writing and Writing about Women.* New York: Harper, 1977.

Jameson, Fredric. "Imaginary and Symbolic in Lacan: Marxism, Psychoanalytic Criticism, and the Problem of the Subject." *YFS* 55/56 (1977): 338–95.

——. *The Political Unconscious: Narrative as a Socially Symbolic Act.* Ithaca: Cornell UP, 1981.

——. "The Politics of Theory: Ideological Positions in the Postmodern Debate." *New German Critique* 33.11.3 (Fall 1984): 53–65.

Jardine, Alice. *Gynesis: Configurations of Woman and Modernity.* Ithaca: Cornell UP, 1985.

——. "Introduction to Julia Kristeva's 'Women's Time.'" *Signs* 7.1 (1981): 5–12.

——. "Pre-Texts for the Transatlantic Feminist." *Feminist Readers,* 220–34.

——. "Theories of the Feminine: Kristeva." *enclitic* 4 (1980): 5–16.

Jardine, Alice, and Paul Smith, eds. *Men in Feminism.* New York: Methuen, 1987.

Johnson, Barbara. *The Critical Difference: Essays in the Contemporary Rhetoric of Reading.* Baltimore: Johns Hopkins UP, 1980.

——. *A World of Difference.* Baltimore: Johns Hopkins UP, 1987.

Jones, Rosalind. "Writing the Body: Toward an Understanding of *l'écriture féminine.*" *Feminist Studies* 7.2 (Summer 1981): 247–63.

Kafka, Franz. *The Great Wall of China: Stories and Reflections.* Trans. Willa Muir and Edwin Muir. New York: Schocken, 1970.

Kamuf, Peggy. "A Double Life (Femmeninism II)." Jardine and Smith 91-97.

——. "Writing Like a Woman." McConnell-Ginet, Borker, and Furman 284–99.

Keohane, Nannerl O., Michelle S. Rosaldo, and Barbara C. Gelpi, eds. *Feminist Theory: A Critique of Ideology.* 1981. Chicago: U of Chicago P, 1982.

Kofman, Sarah. *The Eye of Woman: Woman in Freud's Writing.* Trans. Catherine Porter. Ithaca: Cornell UP, 1985.

Kolodny, Annette. "Some Notes Defining a 'Feminist Literary Criticism.'" *Denver Quarterly* 17.4 (Winter 1983): 40–57.

Korenman, Joan. "The 'Liberation' of Margaret Drabble." *Critique: Studies in Modern Fiction* 21.3 (1980): 61–72.

Kristeva, Julia. *About Chinese Women.* Trans. Anita Barrows. New York: Urizen, 1977.

——. "China, Women, and the Symbolic: An Interview with Julia Kristeva." *Sub-Stance* 13 (1976): 9–18.

——. *Desire in Language: A Semiotic Approach to Literature and Art.* Ed. Leon S. Roudiez. Trans. Thomas Gora, Alice Jardine, and Leon S. Roudiez. New York: Columbia UP, 1980.

——. *Powers of Horror.* Trans. Leon S. Roudiez. New York: Columbia UP, 1982.

——. "Psychoanalysis and the Polis." Trans. Margaret Waller. *Critical Inquiry* 9 (1982): 77–92.

——. *Revolution in Poetic Language.* Trans. Margaret Waller. New York: Columbia UP, 1984.

——. "Woman Can Never Be Defined." Trans. Marilyn August. Marks and Courtivron 165–68.

———. "Women's Time." Trans. Alice Jardine and Harry Blake. *Signs* 7.1 (1981): 13–35.

Krupnick, Mark, ed. *Displacement: Derrida and After*. Bloomington: Indiana UP, 1983.

Lacan, Jacques. *Ecrits*. 2 vols. Paris: Seuil, 1966–71.

———. *Ecrits: A Selection*. Trans. Alan Sheridan. New York: Norton, 1977.

———. *The Four Fundamental Concepts of Psycho-analysis*. Ed. Jacques-Alain Miller. Trans. Alan Sheridan. New York: Norton, 1978.

———. "Seminar on 'The Purloined Letter.'" *YFS* 48 (1972): 39–72.

Lazare, Bernard. *Job's Dungheap: Essays on Jewish Nationalism and Social Revolution, with a Portrait of Bernard Lazare by Charles Peguy*. Trans. Harry Lorin Binsse. New York: Schocken, 1948.

"Letters: More on Hannah Arendt (between Martin Jay and Leon Botstein)." *Partisan Review* 46.2 (1979): 317–18.

"Letters: Remembrance of Things Past (between Lionel Abel and William Phillips on Hannah Arendt)." *Partisan Review* 51.1 (1984): 159–60.

Lewis, C. S. *The Allegory of Love: A Study in Medieval Tradition*. 1936. London: Oxford UP, 1953.

Lewis, Philip. "The Post-structural Condition." *Diacritics* 12.1 (Spring 1982): 2–24.

Libby, Vlastos Marion. "Fate and Femininism in the Novels of Margaret Drabble." *Contemporary Literature* 16.2 (Spring 1975): 175–92.

Literature and Psychoanalysis. The Question of Reading: Otherwise. Ed. Shoshana Felman. *YFS* 55/56 (1977): special issue.

Lydon, Mary. "Foucault and Feminism: A Romance of Many Dimensions." *Humanities in Society* 5.3.4 (1982): 245–56.

———. "*The Story of Adèle H*. or the Insistence of the Letter." *Cream City Review* 7.2 (1982): 33–41.

———. "Translating Duras: 'The Man Seated in the Passage.'" *Contemporary Literature* 24.2 (Summer 1983): 259–75.

Lyotard, Jean-François. "The Differend, The Referent, and the Proper Name." Trans. Georges Van Den Abeele. *Diacritics* 14.3 (Fall 1984): 4–14.

———. "Interview." *Diacritics* 14.3 (Fall 1984): 16–23.

———. *The Postmodern Condition: A Report on Knowledge*. Trans. Geoff Bennington and Brian Massumi. Minneapolis: U of Minnesota P, 1984.

McCarthy, Mary. "The Vita Activa." Rev. of *The Human Condition*, by Hannah Arendt. *On the Contrary*. New York: Farrar, Straus, 1961. 155–64.

McConnell-Ginet, Sally, Ruth Borker, and Nelly Furman. *Women and Language in Literature and Society*. New York: Praeger, 1980.

McKenna, Andrew. "Postmodernism: It s Future Perfect." *Postmodernism and Continental Philosophy*. Ed. Hugh J. Silverman and Donn Welton. *Selected Studies in Phenomenology and Existential Philosophy* 13 (1987): 228–42.

Margaronis, Maria. "The Occupying Passion." Rev. of *The Sea Wall, The Lover, The War*, by Marguerite Duras. *The Nation* 8 November 1986: 493–96.

Marks, Elaine. "Feminisms Wake" *Boundary* 2.12.2 (Winter 1984): 99–110.

———. "Women and Literature in France." *Signs* 3.43 (1978): 832–42.

Marks, Elaine, and Isabelle de Courtivron, eds. *New French Feminisms: An Anthology*. Amherst: U of Massachusetts P, 1980.

Martin, Biddy. "Woman and Modernity: The (Life) Styles of Lou Andreas-Salome." Working Papers No. 5. Milwaukee: U of Wisconsin-Milwaukee, center for Twentieth-Century Studies, Fall 1986.

Maupassant, Guy de. *Le Horla et autres contes cruels*. Paris: Garnier, 1976. Trans. Albert M. C. McMaster et al. *The Horla; Miss Harriet; Little Lucy Roque, and Other Stories*. Vol. 4 of *The Works of Guy de Maupassant*. London: Classic, 1911.

May, Derwent. *Hannah Arendt*. Middlesex: Penguin, 1986.

Mehlman, Jeffrey. *Revolution and Repetition: Marx/Hugo/Balzac*. Berkeley: U of California P, 1977.

―――. *A Structural Study of Autobiography: Proust, Leiris, Sartre, Lévi-Strauss*. Ithaca: Cornell UP, 1974.

Miller, J. Hillis. "The Critic as Host." *Critical Inquiry* 3.3 (1972): 439–47.

Miller, Nancy K. "Parables and Politics: Feminist Criticism in 1986." *Paragraph Feminism*. Ed. Diana Knight. Spec. issue of 8 (October 1986): 40–54.

―――. "Women's Autobiography in France: For a Dialectics of Identification." McConnell-Ginet, Borker, and Furman 258–73.

Milton, John. *Areopagitica and Of Education*. Ed. Michael Davis. London: Macmillan, 1963.

Mitchell, Juliet. *Psychoanalysis and Feminism*. New York: Vintage, 1975.

Mitchell, Juliet, and Jacqueline Rose, eds. *Feminine Sexuality: Jacques Lacan and the* école freudienne. Trans. Jacqueline Rose. New York: Norton, 1982.

Moers, Ellen. *Literary Women*. 1976. New York: Oxford UP, 1985.

Moi, Toril. *Sexual, Textual Politics: Feminist Literary Theory*. London: Methuen, 1985.

Moncrieff, C. K. Scott, and Terence Kilmartin, trans. *Remembrance of Things Past*. By Marcel Proust. 3 vols. New York: Random House, 1981.

Montrelay, Michèle. "Inquiry into Femininity." *m/f* 1 (1978): 83–104.

Moran, Mary Hurley. *Margaret Drabble: Existing Within Structures*. Carbondale: Southern Illinois UP, 1983.

Munk, Erica. "Beyond Anomie Lines: Marguerite Duras and the Art of Suffering." Rev. of *The War, The Little Horses of Tarquinia, The Sailor from Gibraltar, The Ravishing of Lol Stein, The Malady of Death*, by Marguerite Duras. *The Village Voice* 15 July 1986: 47, 50.

Murphy, Carol J. *Alienation and Absence in the Novels of Marguerite Duras*. Lexington, KY: French Forum, 1982.

Myer, Valerie Grosvenor. *Margaret Drabble: Puritanism and Permissiveness*. London: Vision, 1974.

Nelson, Benjamin, ed. *On Creativity and the Unconscious: Papers on the Psychology of Art, Literature, Love, Religion*. Trans. Joan Riviere. New York: Harper, 1958.

Nietzsche, Friedrich. *The Gay Science with a Prelude in Rhymes and an Appendix of Songs*. Trans. Walter Kaufmann. New York: Vintage, 1974.

———. "On Truth and Lie in an Extra-Moral Sense." *Portable Nietzsche*. Trans. and ed. Walter Kaufmann. 1954. Middlesex: Penguin, 1976.

———. *Will to Power*. Trans. Walter Kaufmann and R. J. Hollingdale. New York: Vintage, 1968.

O'Brien, Mary. "Feminist Theory and Dialectical Logic." Keohane, Rosaldo, and Gelpi, 66–112.

———. *The Politics of Reproduction*. London: Routledge, 1981.

O'Donnell, Francis J. "Hannah Arendt." *Humanities* 4.5 (November 1983): 12–13.

Owens, Craig. "The Discourse of Others: Feminism and Postmodern-ism." Foster 57–82.

Patrick, J. Max, ed. and intro. *The Prose of John Milton: Selected and Edited from the Original Texts with Introductions, Notes, Translations, and Accounts of All His Major Writings*. New York: New York UP, 1968.

Proust, Marcel. *A la recherche du temps perdu*. Pleiade ed. 3 vols. Paris: Gallimard, 1954.

Rezzori, Gregor von. *Memoirs of an Anti-Semite*. New York: Viking, 1981.

Rilke, Rainer Maria. *The Notebooks of Malte Laurids Brigge*. Trans. M. D. Herter Norton. New York: Norton, 1964.

Rorty, Richard. "Philosophy as a Kind of Writing: An Essay on Derrida." *New Literary History* (1978): 141–60.

Rose, Ellen Cronan, ed. *Critical Essays on Margaret Drabble*. Boston: G. K. Hall, 1985.

———. "Drabble's *The Middle Ground:* 'Mid-Life' Narrative Strategies" *Critique: Studies in Modern Fiction* 23.3 (Spring 1982): 69–82.

———. *The Novels of Margaret Drabble: Equivocal Figures*. London: Macmillan, 1980.

Sadler, Lynn Veach. *Margaret Drabble*. Boston: Twayne, 1986.

Sarraute, Nathalie. *The Age of Suspicion*. Trans. Maria Jolas. New York: George Braziller, 1963.

Schmidt, Dorey, ed. *Margaret Drabble: Golden Realms*. Edinburg, TX: Pan American U, 1982.

Schor, Naomi. "Introducing Feminism." *Feminism*. Ed. Diana Knight. Spec. issue of *Paragraph* 8 (October 1986): 94–101.

Serres, Michel. *The Parasite*. Trans. Lawrence Schehr. Baltimore: Johns Hopkins UP, 1982.

Showalter, Elaine. "Feminist Criticism in the Wilderness." Abel 9–36.

———. *A Literature of Their Own*. Princeton: Princeton UP, 1977.

———. "Towards a Feminist Poetics." Jacobus et al. 22–41.

Spivak, Gayatri Chakravorty. "Displacement and the Discourse of Woman." Krupnick 169–95.

———. "Finding Feminist Readings: Dante-Yeats." *Social Text* 3 (1980): 73–87.

———. "Three Feminist Readings: McCullers, Drabble, Habermas." *Union Seminary Quarterly Review* 35.1.2 (Fall/Winter 1979–80): 15–34.

———. "Unmaking and Making in *To the Lighthouse*." McConnell-Ginet, Borker, and Furman 310–27.

Sprigge, Elizabeth. *Gertrude Stein: Her Life and Work*. New York: Harper, 1957.

Stein, Gertrude. *The Autobiography of Alice B. Toklas*. New York: Harcourt, 1933.

———. *The Geographical History of America or The Relation of Human Nature to the Human Mind*. 1936. New York: Vintage, 1973.

———. *Look at Me Now and Here I Am: Writing and Lectures, 1909–45*. Ed. Patricia Meyerowitz. Middlesex: Penguin, 1971.

Sterne, Laurence. *Tristram Shandy*. Middlesex: Penguin, 1967.

Suleiman, Susan Rubin. *Subversive Intent: Gender Politics, and the Avant-Garde*. Cambridge: Harvard UP, 1990.

Tison-Braun, Micheline. *Marguerite Duras*. Amsterdam: Rodopi, 1984.

Trinh, T. Minh-ha. *Woman, Native, Other: Writing Postcoloniality and Feminism*. Bloomington: Indiana UP, 1989.

Ulmer, Gregory. *Applied Grammatology: Post(e)-Pedagogy from Jacques Derrida to Joseph Beuys*. Baltimore: Johns Hopkins UP, 1985.

———. "Of a Parodic Tone Recently Adopted in Criticism." *New Literary History* 13.3 (Spring 1982): 543–60.

———. "The Post-Age." *Diacritics* 11.3 (Fall 1981): 39–56.

Walker, Nancy. "Women Drifting: Drabble's *The Waterfall* and Chopin's *The Awakening*." *Denver Quarterly* 17.4 (Winter 1983): 88—96.

Weissberg, Liliane. "Writing on the Wall: Letters of Rahel Varnhagen." *New German Critique* 36.12.3 (Fall 1985): 157–73.

Welty, Eudora. *One Writer's Beginnings*. Cambridge, MA: Harvard UP, 1984.

Wenzel, Helene Vivienne. "The Text as Body/Politics: An Appreciation Of Monique Wittig's Writings in Context." *Feminist Studies* 7.2 (Summer 1981): 264–87.

Wiesel, Elie. *La Nuit*. Paris: Minuit, 1958.

Wilde, Alan. *Horizons of Assent*. Baltimore: Johns Hopkins UP, 1981.

Wilde, Oscar. *Essays by Oscar Wilde*. Ed. Hesketh Pearson. London: Methuen, 1950.

Williamson, Marilyn L. "Toward a Feminist Literary History." *Signs* 10.1 (1984): 136–47.

Wittig, Monique. *Brouillon pour un dictionnaire des amantes*. Paris: Grasset and Fasquelle, 1976. Trans. Monique Wittig and Sande Zeig. *Lesbian Peoples Material for a Dictionary*. New York: Avon, 1979.

———. *Le corps lesbien*. Paris: Minuit, 1973. Trans. David Le Vay. *The Lesbian Body*. New York: Avon, 1976.

———. *Les guerillères*. Paris: Minuit, 1969. Trans. David Le Vay. *Les Guerillères*. New York: Avon, 1973.

———. *L'opopanax*. Paris, Minuit, 1964. Trans. Helen Weaver. *The Opopanax*. Plainfield, VT: Daughters, 1976.

———. "The Point of View: Universal or Particular?" *Feminist Issues* 3.2 (Fall 1983): 63–69.

Wittkower, Rudolf. *Art and Architecture in Italy 1600–1750*. London: Penguin, 1958.

Woolf, Virginia. *Between the Acts*. New York: Harcourt, 1941.
———. *The Waves*. New York: Harcourt, Brace, 1931.
———. *A Writer's Diary*. 1953. New York: Harcourt, 1954.
Young-Bruehl, Elizabeth. *Hannah Arendt: For Love of the World*. New Haven: Yale UP, 1982.

Index

and language, 14–17, 34, 101, 102, 103, 111, 112–13, 124, 128–30, 132; and the law, 110, 125, 128, 134; *The Life of the Mind,* 122, 135; *Men in Dark Times,* 14, 116; and natality, 14–15, 114, 125; and O'Brien, 13–14, 110; *On Revolution,* 13; *Origins of Totalitarianism,* 98, 99, 133; and pariah, 99, 108, 118–19, 121, 124, 132, 135; and parvenu, 99, 109, 112, 118–19, 120, 121, 123, 132, 134; and Plotinus, 103, 125; and the polis, 13, 110, 124, 128; and the postmodern, 117, 126, 132; and the preface, 100–101, 106, 108; and Proust, 116; and the private realm, 12–15, 110, 111, 114, 126; and the public realm, 12–15, 110, 111, 114, 125, 126, 129; *Rahel Varnhagen,* 12, 14, 99–101, 103–13, 116, 117, 118–19, 121, 123–24; and reader, reading, 16, 100, 104, 106, 112, 114, 116, 123, 125, 131; and remembering, 15–17, 100; and Robinson, E. A., 107; and the schlemiel, 108–9, 119, 120, 122; and self, 99, 102, 104, 112; and the social realm, 14, 126–28; and stories (storytelling), 14–17, 100, 103, 104, 116, 117, 130, 131, 132, 136; and the symbolic order, 11–12, 111; and theory, 13, 14, 98, 124, 132; and thinking (*la vita contemplativa*), 11, 14, 16, 98, 99, 100, 102, 103, 104, 114–15, 116, 117, 122, 124, 131, 132–34, 135; and women, 11, 12, 13, 101, 108, 109, 110, 111, 112, 113, 118, 121–22, 124, 125, 128, 130, 135–36; and the women's movement (the Woman Problem), 12–13, 108, 111; and words, 15, 108, 110, 125, 127–28, 130, 134, 135, 136; and world (*amor mundi*), 11, 12, 13, 14, 17, 19, 97, 99, 104, 107, 112, 116, 121, 124, 126, 131, 132, 135; and the worldless, 13, 24, 99, 112, 124; and writing, 14, 17, 97, 99, 100,

101–3, 104, 105, 106, 107, 109, 112, 116, 118, 121, 123–24, 126, 130, 131, 132, 135, 136
Autobiography, 7, 8, 25, 41, 42, 130. *See also* Arendt, Hannah

Bacon, Francis, 34
Barnes, Djuna, 4
Barthes, Roland, 5. *See also* Arendt, Hannah; Duras, Marguerite
Baudrillard, Jean, 126. *See also* Arendt, Hannah, and the social realm
Baumbach, Jonathan, 4
Beckett, Samuel, 29, 67, 73–74
Bedford, Sybille. *See* Arendt, Hannah
Beginning, 35, 42, 68. *See also* Arendt, Hannah; Stein, Gertrude
Benjamin, Walter, 16, 130. *See also* Arendt, Hannah
Between, 2, 3, 8, 19, 23, 27, 28, 30, 33–34, 39, 52, 53, 54, 57, 61, 66, 67, 69, 74, 85, 94, 102, 124, 125, 126. *See also* Arendt, Hannah; In-between, the
Bildungsroman, 7. *See also* Arendt, Hannah
Biography. *See* Arendt, Hannah
Bloom, Harold, 86
Body, the, 1, 5, 6, 10, 128. *See also* Duras, Marguerite
Bray, Barbara. *See* Duras, Marguerite
Brontë, Charlotte, 47
Brooke-Rose, Christine, 4, 24
Burke, Kenneth, 92
Butor, Michel, 38–39

Callahan, Anne, 29
Chaplin, Charlie, 119
Choice. *See* Drabble, Margaret
Cixous, Hélène, 6–7, 10, 26, 140n.5
Clément, Catherine, 6, 11–12, 19, 128–29, 130
Closure, 2, 8, 21, 34
Colette, 29
Comic, the. *See* Drabble, Margaret

and experience, 27–28, 31, 32, 71, 77–78, 80, 94, 95; and experiment, 24, 27–28, 32, 33, 34, 71; and femininity, 27, 29, 77, 85; and feminism, 24, 29; *La femme du Ganges,* 77; and film, 28, 29; and forgetting, 26, 28, 32, 33, 34, 69, 71, 75, 76, 78, 79, 80, 85, 89, 95; and Freud, 25, 71, 77, 88, 90; and Gauthier, 24, 25, 27; and Heine, 93–94; *Hiroshima mon amour,* 28, 30, 31, 32, 69–74, 79–80, 95, 100; and history, 30, 31, 32, 33, 34, 69–72, 75, 80, 85, 86, 95; and *hors* (outside), 82–83, 84, 89, 93; and the image, 26, 69, 85, 89; *India Song,* 30, 33; and invention, 26, 28, 31, 33, 71, 77, 80; and irony, 91–92, 93; and Jews, 30–32, 92–95; and Lacan, 25, 77, 83, 89, 90; and language, 34, 78, 80, 88; and the letter, 30, 76–77, 83–84, 95, 139n.1 (chap. 3); and C. S. Lewis, 91, 92; and loss, 25, 75, 76, 83; *Maladie de la mort,* 95; and Maupassant, (*Horla*), 89–90, 92, 95; and men, 29, 34; *Moderato Cantabile,* 27; and modernism, 33; and the nebbish, 93; *Outside,* 32; and the pariah, 82, 83, 93–94; *Les parleuses,* 24; and postmodernism, 33, 71; and Proust, 73, 83, 84, 85, 86–89, 94; *Le ravissement de Lol V. Stein,* 24, 27, 31, 32, 33, 76–79, 139n.1 (chap. 3); and reader, reading, 25–26, 27, 28, 30, 32, 33, 85, 86, 88, 89; and remembering, 32, 34, 71, 76, 79, 80, 87, 95; and repetition, 28, 31, 74, 76, 77–78, 95; and Resnais, 28, 70; and Rezzori, ("Troth"), 92–93; and the schlemiel, 93–94; and story (*l'histoire*), 26, 30, 33, 34, 69–72, 74–75, 77, 79–80, 85, 86, 89, 93, 95; and the unconscious, 69, 78, 86, 90; *Le viceconsul,* 29, 31–32, 80–95; and Eli Wiesel, 31; and women writers, 24, 27–29, 32; and wordplay (*jeu de mot*), 77, 91; and words (names),

27, 30–32, 33, 34, 69, 70, 75–78, 79, 80, 83–84, 89, 93, 94, 95; and writing, 25–29, 32, 33, 34, 69, 71, 76, 77, 78–79, 80, 85, 86, 95

Edwards, Lee R., 2
Endings (open, unfinished), 2, 21, 34, 35, 38, 42, 54, 77, 116, 136. *See also* Drabble, Margaret
Envoi. *See* Drabble, Margaret
Essay, 7, 34. *See also* Arendt, Hannah; Drabble, Margaret; Meditation
Essentialism, 6, 7, 9
Experience, 2, 8, 9, 10, 11, 17, 24, 34, 53, 130, 131. *See also* Arendt, Hannah; Drabble, Margaret; Duras, Marguerite
Experimental writing, 2, 3–5, 8, 10, 24, 32, 34, 53, 131, 136. *See also* Arendt, Hannah; Drabble, Margaret; Duras, Marguerite
Exile, 9, 11, 125, 128. *See also* Arendt, Hannah; Duras, Marguerite

Fate. *See* Drabble, Margaret
Fates, the. *See* Drabble, Margaret
Federman, Raymond, 4
Femininity, 3, 5, 6, 7, 29, 129. *See also* Arendt, Hannah; Drabble, Margaret; Duras, Marguerite
Feminism, 1, 2, 3, 8, 9, 10, 12, 130, 131. *See also* French feminism; Women writers
Feminist literary studies, 1–11,
Fiction Collective, 4
Film, 63. *See also* Duras, Marguerite
Flaubert, Gustav, 22–23
Forgetting, 100, 135. *See also* Duras, Marguerite
Foucault, Michel, 5, 25
Fraser, Nancy, 14, 127. *See also* Arendt, Hannah, and the social realm
Freedom, 2, 9, 57, 68. *See also* Arendt, Hannah
French, Marilyn, 8
French feminism, 5, 6